# Doctor Mozart Music Theory Workbook
## Answers for Level 2 a

GW00383388

**Level 2A**

Version 1.1.0
or higher.

Ledger notes
Whole steps up and down
The C, F, and G major scales
Eighth notes
Dotted half notes
Primary and secondary accents
Time signatures

**2A**

**Level 2B**

Version 1.0.5
or higher.

Major and minor 2nds and 3rds
Perfect 4ths and 5ths
White key accidentals
Major and minor triads
Primary triads on I, IV, and V in C, F, and G major
2/8, 3/8, and 4/8 time signatures
Eighth rests

**2B**

**Level 2C**

Version 1.0.5
or higher.

Major and minor 6ths and 7ths
Unisons and octaves
Key signatures
The D major and B flat major scales
Minor scales and primary triads
16th notes and rests
Dotted quarter notes

**2C**

**Level 3**

Version 1.0.1
or higher.

Key signatures up to 4 flats
    and 5 sharps
The circle of 5ths
Melodic minor scales
Intervals on ledger notes
Triad inversions
Transposition
Cadences

Dotted eighth notes
Common time and cut time
Triplets
Compound time signatures
Upbeats
Adding rests to complete a bar
Repetition and sequences
Musical terminology

**3**

Version 1.1.0

Doctor Mozart Music Theory Workbook, Answers for Level 2 & 3.   © MMVIII, MMXV  Machiko and Paul Christopher Musgrave.   Published by April Avenue Music.   www.DoctorMozart.com

# For Parents and Teachers

This answer book is intended to make marking and correcting easier for you.

While using this book, you may wonder why it does not provide answers for some questions. The reason is that those questions are creative exercises that can be completed in various different ways, and there is no single right answer.

You might also have noticed that the actual Doctor Mozart workbooks are printed in color, which makes them more attractive for children. In contrast, this answer book is printed in black and white, to make it more affordable.

Over the years, the Doctor Mozart workbooks have occasionally been updated. For that reason, each workbook has a version number printed at the bottom of its first page. To see if your workbooks match this answer book, simply look at the version numbers printed in this book's table of contents. Normally, the current version of this answer book will match the current versions of the workbooks.

We hope you find this answer book helpful.

Thank you for choosing Doctor Mozart.

# Doctor Mozart® Music Theory Workbook

## In-Depth Piano Theory Fun for Music Lessons and Home Schooling

**Level 2A** – Contents

We will help you learn and remember each lesson.

2 A

Hi! I'm Doctor Mozart.

Highly Effective for Beginners Learning a Musical Instrument.

Doctor Mozart workbooks are filled with friendly cartoon characters. They make it fun to learn music theory in-depth. And in-depth music theory knowledge is essential for children learning a musical instrument. Use Doctor Mozart workbooks by themselves or with other teaching materials. Use them for music lessons and for home schooling.

The authors, Machiko and Paul Musgrave, are both graduates of Juilliard. Machiko has taught piano and theory at Soai University in Japan. Paul is an Associate of the Royal Conservatory of Music. The authors hope you enjoy using this book!

**Copyright laws protect the right of authors and publishers to earn a living from their work. Please respect these laws, and pay for the books you use and enjoy. Photocopying or reproducing this book in any manner may lead to prosecution.**

Many thanks to Kevin Musgrave for his meticulous proof-reading and insightful suggestions.
Created by Machiko and Paul Christopher Musgrave. Illustrated by Machiko Yamane Musgrave.

1.1

# Grand Staff Notes
### Review

Write the words and sentences that can help you remember the grand staff note names.

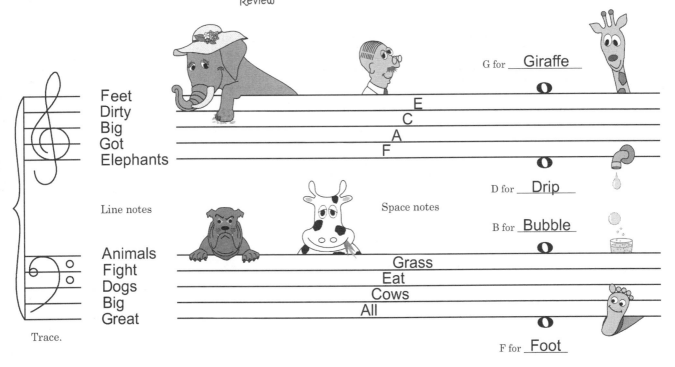

Feet
Dirty
Big
Got
Elephants

Line notes

Animals
Fight
Dogs
Big
Great

Space notes

E
C
A
F

Grass
Eat
Cows
All

G for Giraffe

D for Drip

B for Bubble

F for Foot

Trace.

Hint: Elephants Got Big Dirty Feet. FACE. Great Big Dogs Fight Animals. All Cows Eat Grass. Foot, Bubble, Drip, Giraffe.

Make a grand staff. Write all the white key space notes on the grand staff.

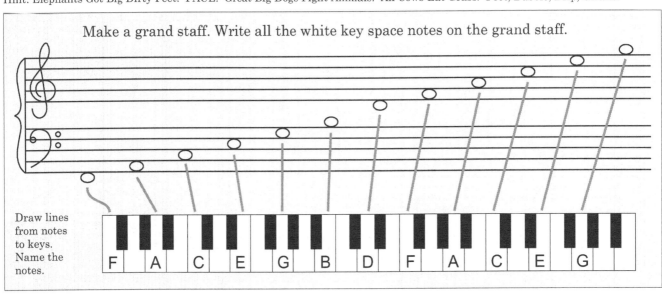

Draw lines from notes to keys. Name the notes.

F A C E G B D F A C E G

Name each printed note. After each printed note, write two other notes that have the same name.

3 of each note

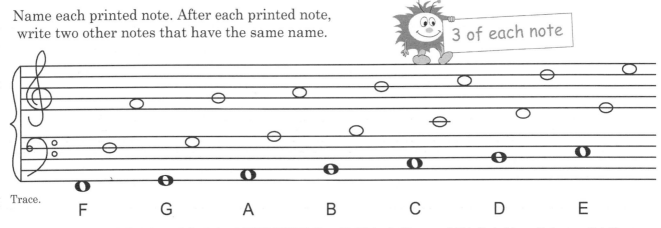

Trace.

F G A B C D E

# Grand Staff Quiz

Write the correct clef on each staff.

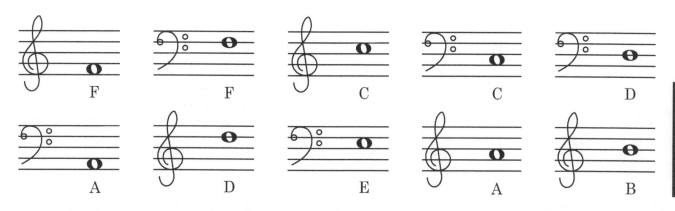

F    F    C    C    D

A    D    E    A    B

**2A**

Always start by making a grand staff.

After each printed note, write a note in the bass staff that looks similar. Name the notes.

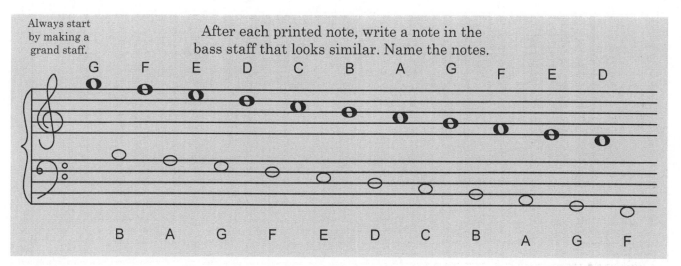

G F E D C B A G F E D

B A G F E D C B A G F

Write 4 different F sharps, 4 G flats, and 3 C sharps.

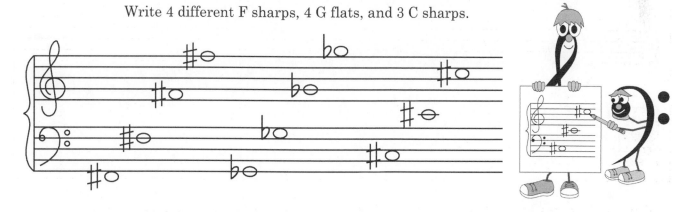

Below, if the red arrow points *up*, write a note that is one semitone *above* the given note.
If the red arrow points *down*, write a note that is one semitone *below* the given note.

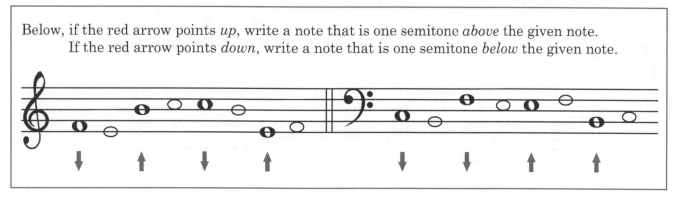

# Review GRAND STAFF & Accidentals

Name the notes.

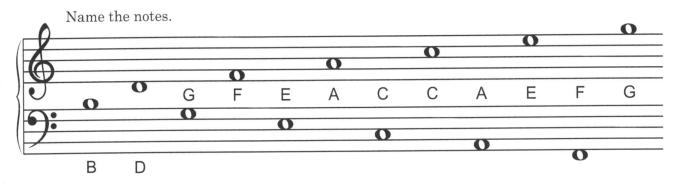

G F E A C C A E F G

B D

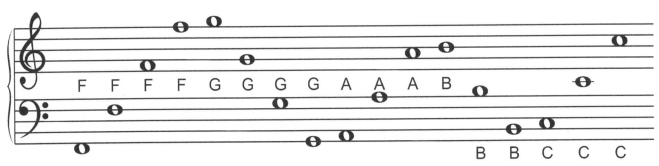

F F F F G G G A A A B

B B C C C

Draw lines from notes to keys.

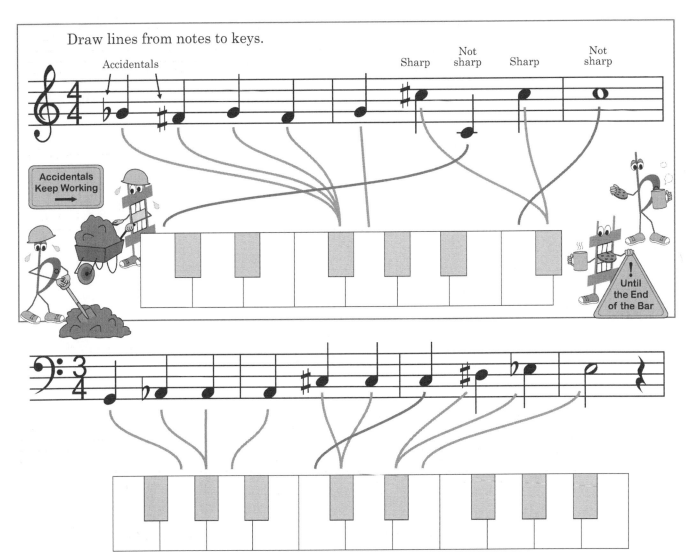

Accidentals

Sharp    Not sharp    Sharp    Not sharp

Accidentals Keep Working →

Until the End of the Bar

# What are Ledger Notes?

Some notes are too high
or low for the staff.
To write these notes,
we need ledger lines.

Draw lines from notes to keys.
Name the notes on the keyboard.

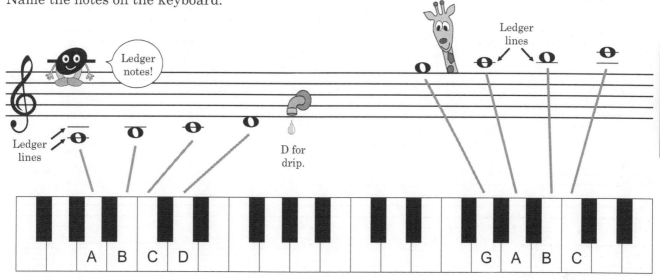

2
A

Ledger
notes!

Ledger
lines

Ledger
lines

D for
drip.

A B C D          G A B C

B for
bubble.

F for
foot

C D E F          B C D E

Below, two notes are marked with a red X.
This is because they each have an extra ledger line.
Write an X at any similar mistakes you find.

Ledger lines and staff
lines should be
the same distance apart.

Do not write
this line.

Do not
write this line.

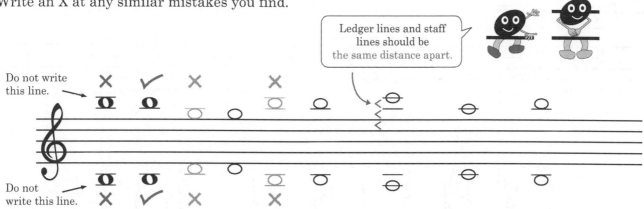

Trace only the correct notes.

Write some ledger notes on your own.

Doctor Mozart Music Theory Workbook, Answers for Level 2 & 3.   © MMVIII, MMXV  Machiko and Paul Christopher Musgrave.   Published by April Avenue Music.   www.DoctorMozart.com

# Treble Staff Ledger Notes

Name these notes.

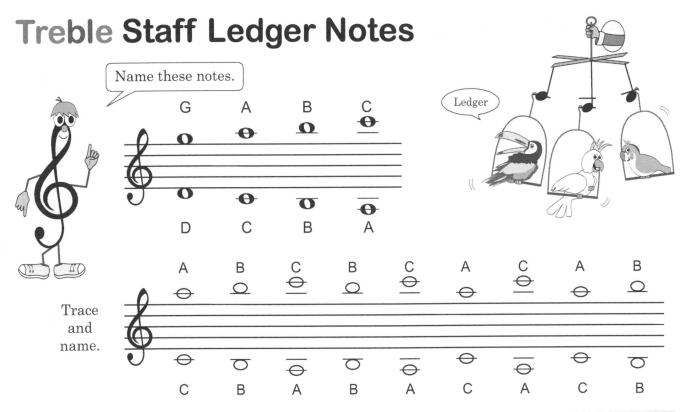

Trace and name.

Write the notes. Name them.

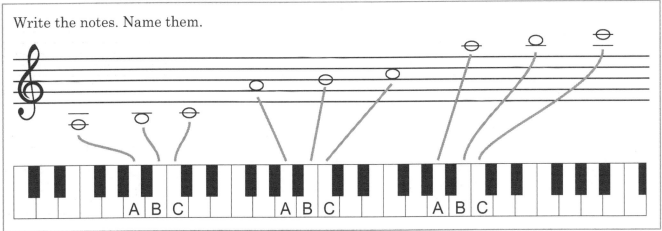

Draw lines from notes to keys.

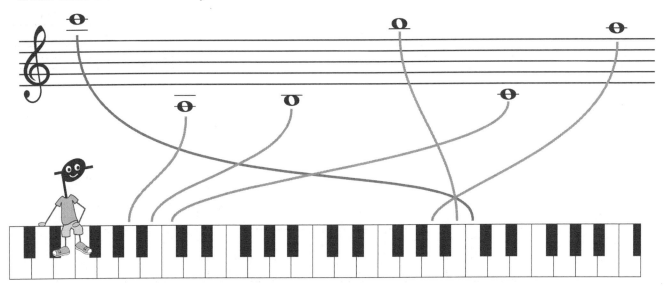

Doctor Mozart Music Theory Workbook, Answers for Level 2 & 3.  © MMVIII, MMXV  Machiko and Paul Christopher Musgrave.    Published by April Avenue Music.    www.DoctorMozart.com

# Bass Staff Ledger Notes

Name the notes.

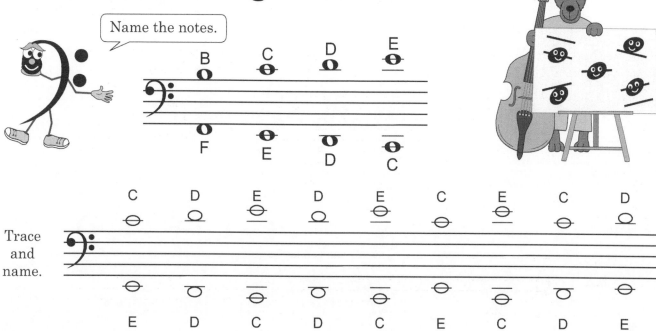

Trace
and
name.

Write a note at the end of each line. Name each note.

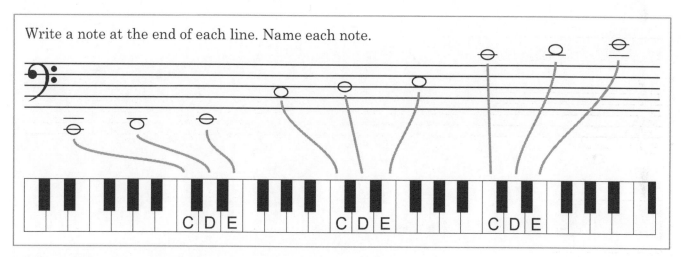

C D E     C D E     C D E

Draw lines from notes to keys.

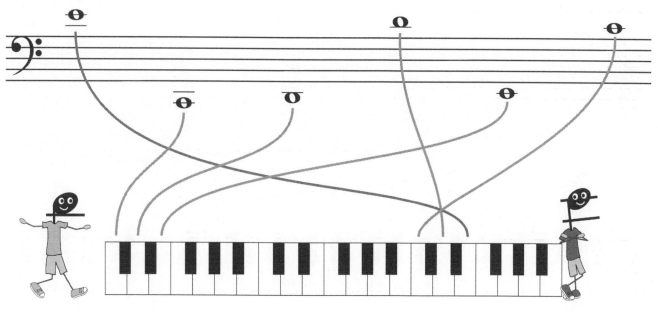

Doctor Mozart Music Theory Workbook, Answers for Level 2 & 3.  © MMVIII, MMXV  Machiko and Paul Christopher Musgrave.    Published by April Avenue Music.    www.DoctorMozart.com

# Ledger Note EXERCISE

Write a note for each letter. If the arrow points up, write the note *above* the staff. If the arrow points down, write the note *below* the staff.

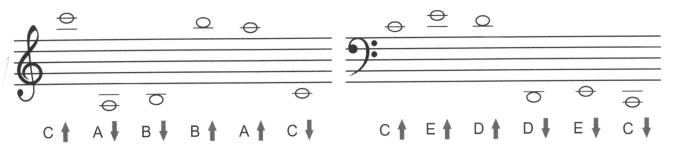

Next, trace and name each note. Draw lines from notes to keys.

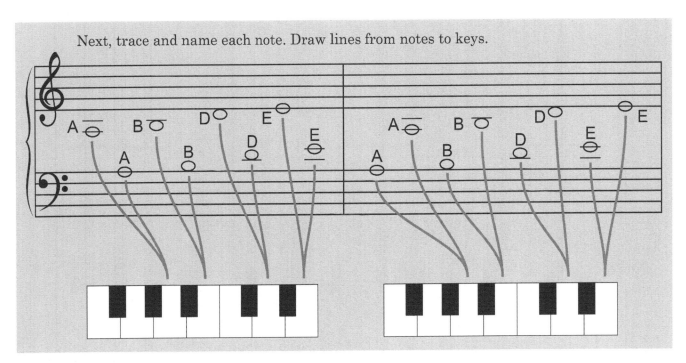

Write 6 different ledger notes. Draw lines from notes to keys. Name each note.

These are just 2 example answers.

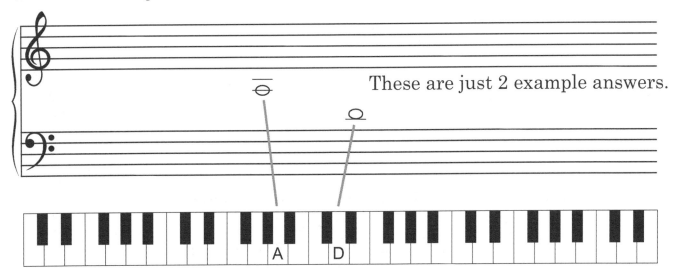

Doctor Mozart Music Theory Workbook, Answers for Level 2 & 3.  © MMVIII, MMXV  Machiko and Paul Christopher Musgrave.    Published by April Avenue Music.    www.DoctorMozart.com

# Musical Sign Quiz

Draw lines to match each sign with its name and meaning.

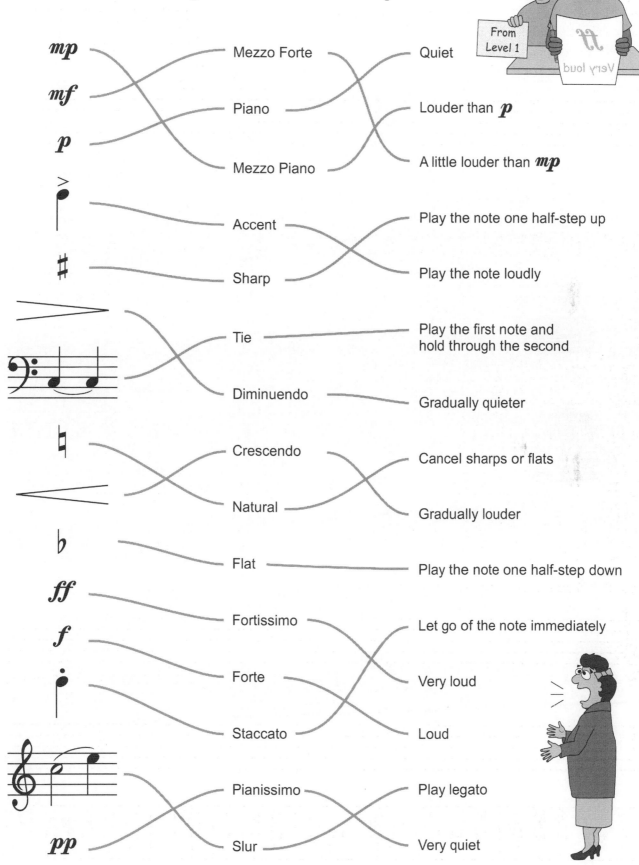

**mp**

**mf**

**p**

Mezzo Forte — Quiet

Piano — Louder than **p**

Mezzo Piano — A little louder than **mp**

Accent — Play the note one half-step up

Sharp — Play the note loudly

Tie — Play the first note and hold through the second

Diminuendo — Gradually quieter

Crescendo — Cancel sharps or flats

Natural — Gradually louder

Flat — Play the note one half-step down

**ff** — Fortissimo — Let go of the note immediately

**f** — Forte — Very loud

Staccato — Loud

Pianissimo — Play legato

**pp** — Slur — Very quiet

From Level 1

ff — Very loud

2
A

# Time *Signature*

In 2 / 4 time:

There are 2 beats in each bar.

Each beat is a quarter note.

Each bar has __2__ beats.

Each beat is a ____quarter____ note.

Next, are the beats half notes or quarter notes? Circle the number in each time signature that tells you. Fill each bar with quarter notes.

Number the beats.

In 2 / 2 time:

There are 2 beats in each bar.

Each beat is a half note.

Each bar has __2__ beats.

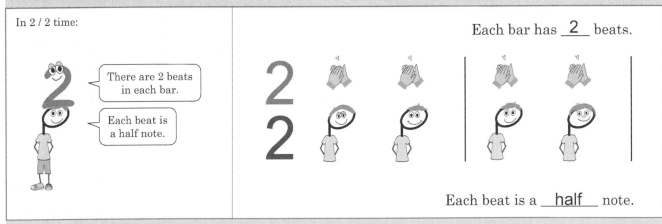

Each beat is a __half__ note.

Next, are the beats half notes or quarter notes? Circle the numbers that tell you. Fill each bar with half notes. Number the beats.

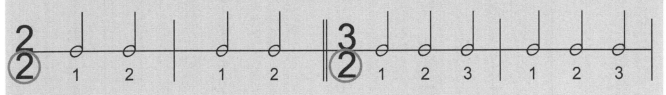

Number the beats.

A __4__ on the bottom means each *quarter* note gets __1__ beat.

A __2__ on the bottom means that each *half* note gets __1__ beat.

A 4 on the bottom means each ____quarter____ note gets 1 beat.

Doctor Mozart Music Theory Workbook, Answers for Level 2 & 3.  © MMVIII, MMXV  Machiko and Paul Christopher Musgrave.    Published by April Avenue Music.    www.DoctorMozart.com

# Steady Beats

Accent the first beat in each bar.
Number the beats.

Write an ampersand (&) under any notes that are between the beats.

Tap and count.

Fill each bar with *quarter* notes. Number the beats. Accent the first beat of each bar.

| $\frac{3}{2}$ | means 3 | half | note beats in each bar. |
|---|---|---|---|
| $\frac{3}{4}$ | means 3 | quarter | note beats in each bar. |
| $\frac{2}{2}$ | means 2 | half | note beats in each bar. |
| $\frac{2}{4}$ | means 2 | quarter | note beats in each bar. |

Write an X under any bar that has the wrong number of beats.

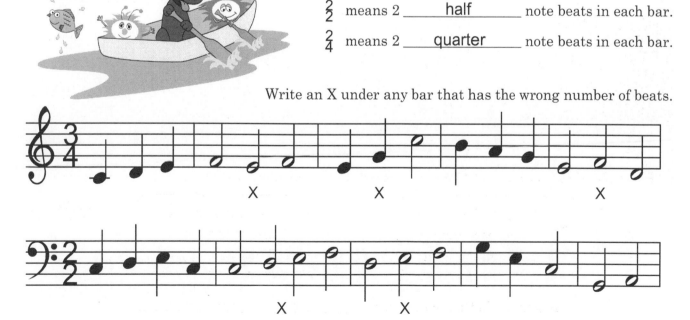

Doctor Mozart Music Theory Workbook, Answers for Level 2 & 3.   © MMVIII, MMXV  Machiko and Paul Christopher Musgrave.   Published by April Avenue Music.   www.DoctorMozart.com

# LEDGER *Note Quiz*

Fill both the treble and bass staffs
with quarter, half, and whole notes.

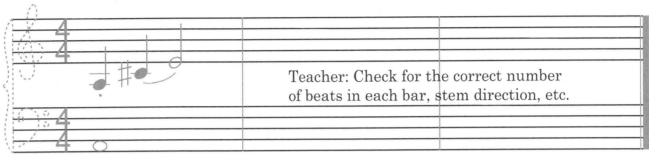

Teacher: Check for the correct number
of beats in each bar, stem direction, etc.

Number
the beats.    1

Include some ledger notes, slurs, ties, accents, accidentals, and staccato quarter notes.

Make a grand staff. Write a 2 / 2 time signature. Then do the same as above.

Teacher: Check for the correct number
of beats in each bar, stem direction, etc.

Fill
in the
blanks.

$\frac{2}{2}$ means there are ___2___ ___half___ note beats in each bar.

$\frac{3}{2}$ means there are ___3___ ___half___ note beats in each bar.

Write 6 different ledger notes. Include some accidentals. Draw lines from notes to keys.

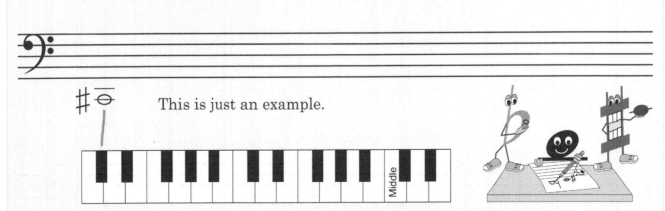

This is just an example.

Middle

Doctor Mozart Music Theory Workbook, Answers for Level 2 & 3.  © MMVIII, MMXV  Machiko and Paul Christopher Musgrave.    Published by April Avenue Music.    www.DoctorMozart.com

# Ledger Note FUN

Write 6 different ledger notes: 3 above the staff, and 3 below. Include some accidentals.

This is just an example.

Draw lines.

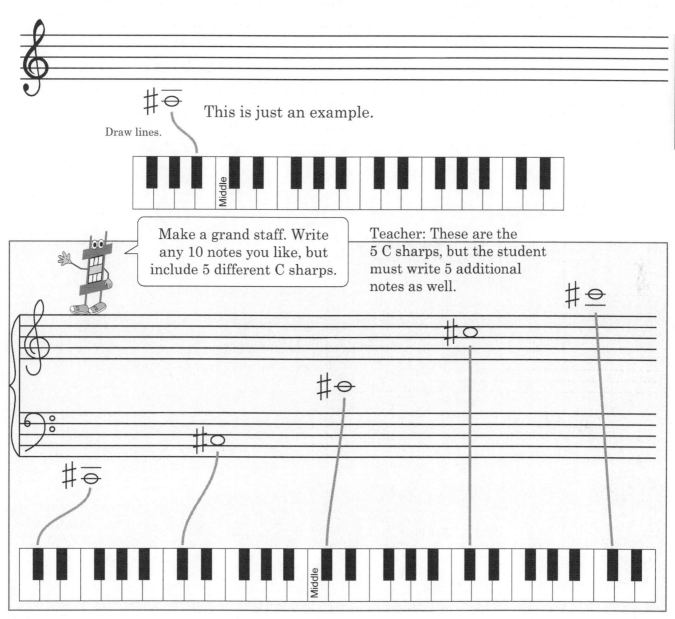

Make a grand staff. Write any 10 notes you like, but include 5 different C sharps.

Teacher: These are the 5 C sharps, but the student must write 5 additional notes as well.

Make a grand staff. Near middle C, write a note for each letter – two different ways.

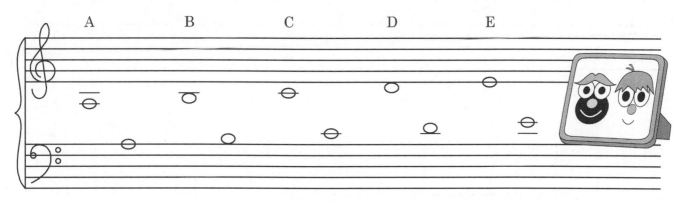

A    B    C    D    E

# 1 Whole = 1 Half + 1 Half

If you want to share a muffin equally with a friend, break it into two equal pieces.

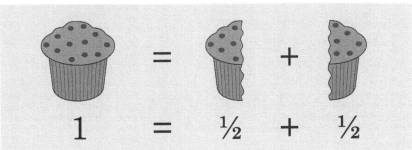

$$1 = \frac{1}{2} + \frac{1}{2}$$

Then you can eat half the muffin and your friend can eat the other half.

The word *half* is also written as ½.

Answer with a note:

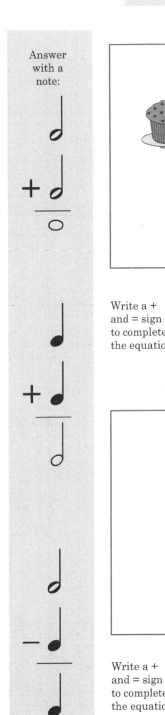

What kind of note is half as long as a *whole* note?

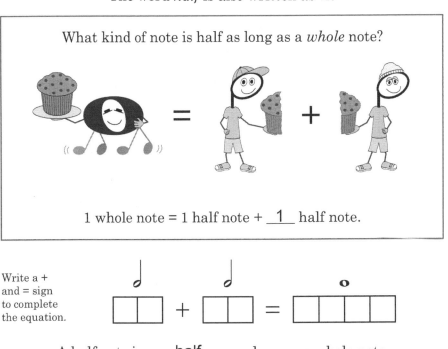

1 whole note = 1 half note + __1__ half note.

How many quarter note beats? Write a number:

Write a +
and = sign
to complete
the equation.

A half note is ____half____ as long as a whole note.

What kind of note is half as long as a *half* note?

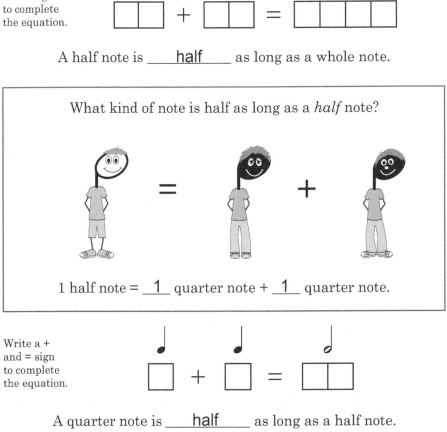

1 half note = __1__ quarter note + __1__ quarter note.

Write a +
and = sign
to complete
the equation.

A quarter note is ____half____ as long as a half note.

# Staccato & Dotted Notes

*Staccato* notes and *dotted* notes are not the same.

If you see a dot *above* or *below* a note, like this ♩ then the note is **staccato**.
Let go of that note immediately after you play it.

A note is ___staccato___ if there is a dot above or below it.

Let go of that note ___immediately___ after you play it.

If you see a dot *after* a note like this ♩. then the note is *not* staccato.
Instead, it is called a **dotted note**. It should be held *longer*.

A dotted note should be held ___longer___.

Below, circle the notes that should be held longer.

Trace the gray dotted half notes.

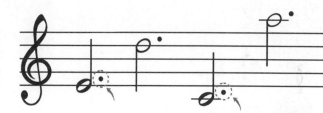

When the note head is on a *space*, the dot should be written in the *same* space.

When the note head is on a *line*, the dot should be written in the space *above*.

Draw some dotted half notes. If you see an arrow pointing up, write the note above the staff.
If you see an arrow pointing down, write the note below the staff.

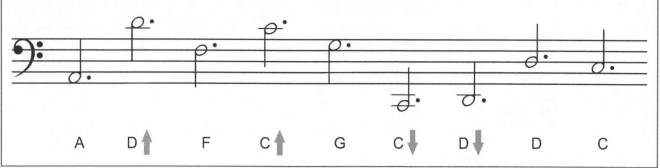

A   D⬆   F   C⬆   G   C⬇   D⬇   D   C

Doctor Mozart Music Theory Workbook, Answers for Level 2 & 3.   © MMVIII, MMXV  Machiko and Paul Christopher Musgrave.   Published by April Avenue Music.   www.DoctorMozart.com

# Dotted Half Note Chocolate

Half Note Henry          Quarter Note Quincy          Dotted Half Note Doreen

Henry can eat __2__ pieces of chocolate. Quincy can eat __1__. Doreen can eat __3__.

Draw the chocolate squares.

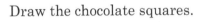

Henry's chocolate          Half of Henry's chocolate          Doreen's chocolate

Write notes to show how much chocolate is eaten by Henry, Quincy, and Doreen.

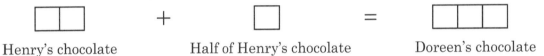

Draw lines to match the chocolate with the notes.

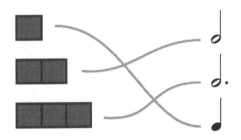

Next, draw some chocolate squares to show how long the notes are.

Write + signs to complete each equation.

☐ + ☐ + ☐ = ☐☐☐

♩ + ♩ + ♩ = ♩.

__3__ quarter notes equal 1 dotted half note.

Next, write each answer as a single note.

Doctor Mozart Music Theory Workbook, Answers for Level 2 & 3.  © MMVIII, MMXV Machiko and Paul Christopher Musgrave.   Published by April Avenue Music.   www.DoctorMozart.com

# Dot Time

Draw bar lines.
Number the beats.

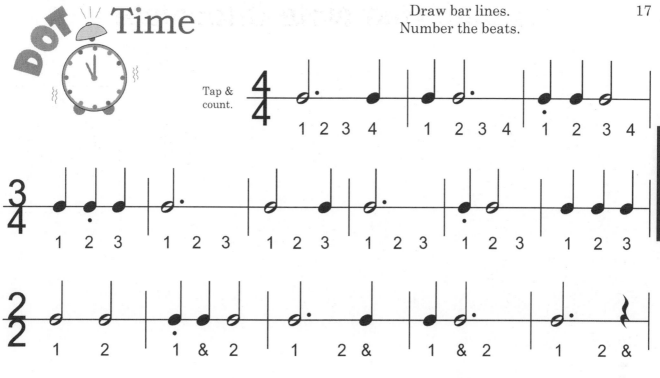

Tap &
count.

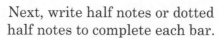

Next, write half notes or dotted
half notes to complete each bar.

Include some ledger notes.

Teacher: Any pitch is fine, but check the time values.

Number
the beats.

Tap and count.

# Quarter Notes *Walk*. Eighth Notes RUN.

This chocolate equation reminds us that 2 quarter notes are as long as 1 __half__ note.

Trace these notes. Write a + and = sign to make a note equation.

♩ + ♩ = ♩

**Quarter notes** usually go at a medium walking speed.

**Half notes** go slower, like slow skating.

Eighth notes are faster, like a running bird.

Trace    ♪ + ♪ = ♪

Two eighth notes together get one quarter note beat.

= 

Eighth notes have a flag, a stem, and a filled-in head. →

Trace the arrows.

**Two** eighth notes last as long as __1__ **quarter note.**

One eighth note is __half__ as long as 1 quarter note.

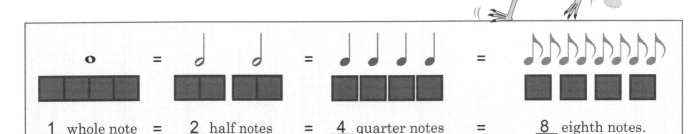

__1__ whole note  =  __2__ half notes  =  __4__ quarter notes  =  __8__ eighth notes.

Answer with a single note.

♪ + ♪ = ♩

♪ + ♪ + ♪ + ♪ = ♩

♪ + ♪ + ♩ = ♩

♪ + ♪ + ♪ + ♪ + ♪ + ♪ + ♪ + ♪ = o

♪ + ♪ + ♪ + ♪ + ♪ + ♪ + ♩ = o

♪ + ♪ + ♪ + ♪ + ♩ = o

Doctor Mozart Music Theory Workbook, Answers for Level 2 & 3.   © MMVIII, MMXV  Machiko and Paul Christopher Musgrave.     Published by April Avenue Music.    www.DoctorMozart.com

# 2 Eighth Notes = 1 Quarter Note

Trace this:

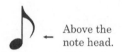

Two __eighth__ notes are as long as one quarter note.

Answer with a single note:

Tap these eighth notes with your right hand while you tap the quarter notes with your left. Count aloud.

---

# Flags and Beams

Eighth notes can have either separate flags, or connecting beams. Trace these notes.

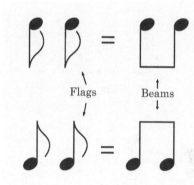

When the stem points up, the flag ends *above* the note head.

← Above the note head.

Trace these notes. Draw the missing stems and flags.

When the stem points down, the flag ends *below* the note head.

← Below the note head.

Trace these notes. Draw the missing stems and flags.

Flags ← → Beams

Flags are always written to the right of the note stem.

---

Below, draw beams across each group of four notes. If *most* of the stems would normally point up, then *all* the stems should point up when joined by a beam.*

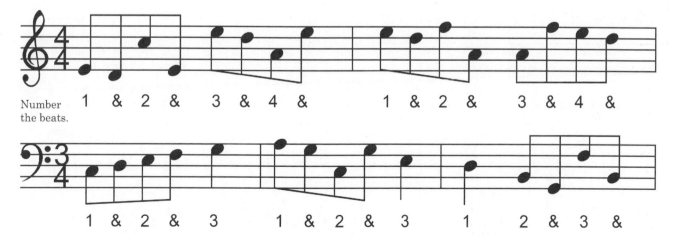

Number the beats.    1 & 2 & 3 & 4 &    1 & 2 & 3 & 4 &

1 & 2 & 3    1 & 2 & 3    1    2 & 3 &

*What if half of the notes would normally point up, and the other half would point down? Then follow the stem direction of the note that is furthest from the middle line.

Doctor Mozart Music Theory Workbook, Answers for Level 2 & 3.  © MMVIII, MMXV Machiko and Paul Christopher Musgrave.    Published by April Avenue Music.    www.DoctorMozart.com

# Meter and Accents

**Meter** is the number of beats in each bar.

Duple meter means <u>2</u> beats in each bar.
Triple meter means <u>3</u> beats per bar.
Quadruple meter means <u>4</u> beats per bar.

The **top** number of the time signature
tells you whether the meter is

<u>duple</u> **(**e.g. **2**/4 time), or

<u>triple</u> (e.g. **3**/4 time), or

<u>quadruple</u> (e.g. **4**/4 time).

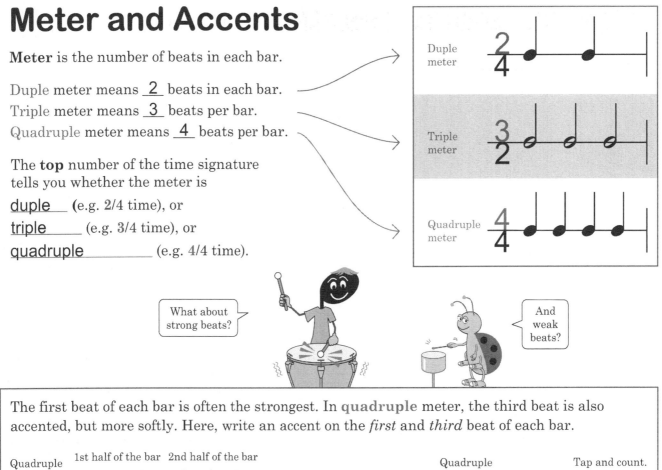

The first beat of each bar is often the strongest. In **quadruple** meter, the third beat is also
accented, but more softly. Here, write an accent on the *first* and *third* beat of each bar.

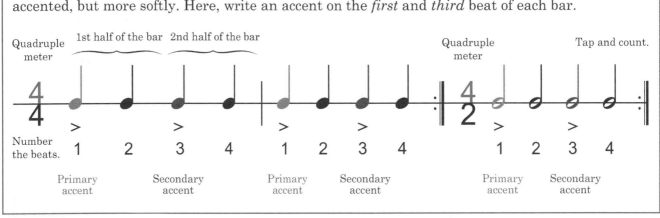

The <u>primary</u> accent is on the first beat. The <u>secondary</u> accent is on the third beat.
Secondary accents occur halfway through each bar in <u>quadruple</u> meter.

The weakest notes of all are the ones *between* beats. We count them with words like *and,* or
*potato,* or *necessary,* or anything that seems to fit. Here, tap and count, using the words shown.

Doctor Mozart Music Theory Workbook, Answers for Level 2 & 3.  © MMVIII, MMXV  Machiko and Paul Christopher Musgrave.    Published by April Avenue Music.    www.DoctorMozart.com

# Eighth Note Rhythm Fun

Trace the gray notes. Write eighth notes to complete each bar.

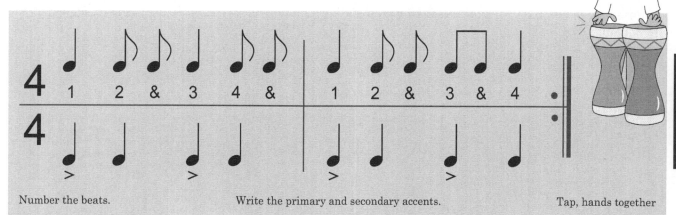

Number the beats.

Write the primary and secondary accents.

Tap, hands together

Triple meter.

There are no secondary accents in triple or duple meter.

Next, do the same as above, but write *1 potato, 2 potato* to count the beats.

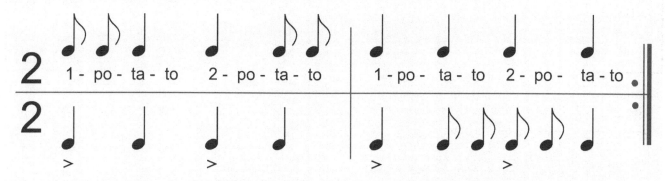

Number the beats. Write the accents.

# Ledger DRILL

Draw the bar lines.
Name the notes.

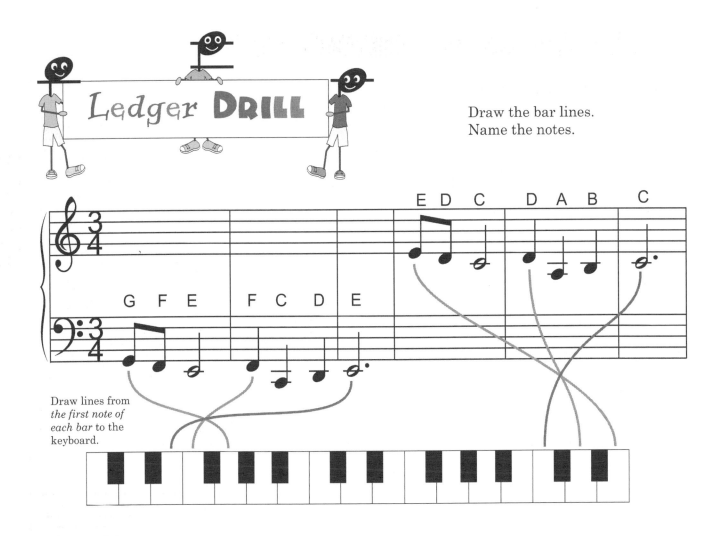

Draw lines from *the first note of each bar* to the keyboard.

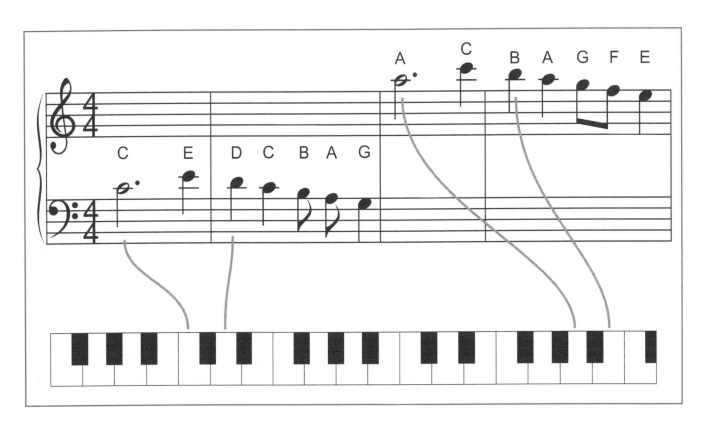

# RHYTHM ON THE GRAND STAFF

Fill each bar with notes – in both staffs.

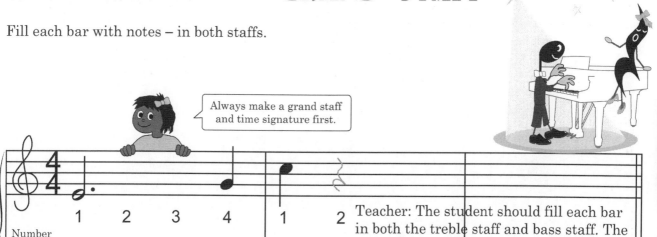

Always make a grand staff and time signature first.

Number the beats.

1   2   3   4   |   1   2

Teacher: The student should fill each bar in both the treble staff and bass staff. The beats in one staff should be aligned with the corresponding beats in the other staff.

Number.   1   2   3   &   4   |   1   &   2

Include some ledger notes, eighth notes, dotted half notes, and quarter rests.

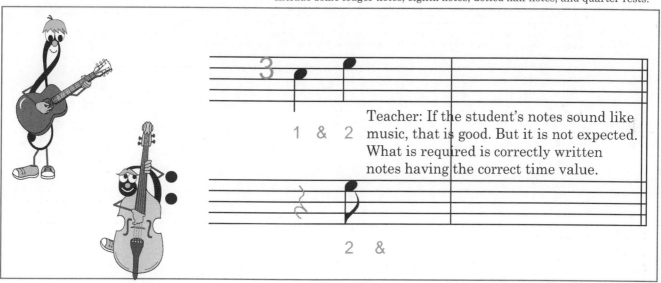

1   &   2

Teacher: If the student's notes sound like music, that is good. But it is not expected. What is required is correctly written notes having the correct time value.

2   &

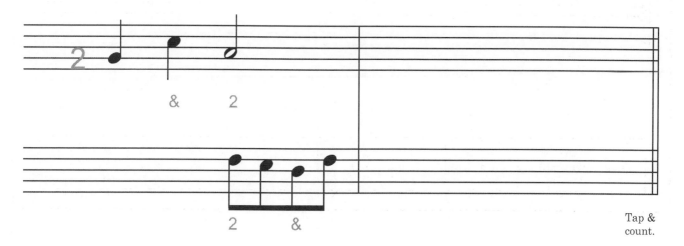

&   2

2   &

Tap & count.

# Chromatic?

For each pair of notes, name the white key first.
Then use the *same* letter to name the black key.

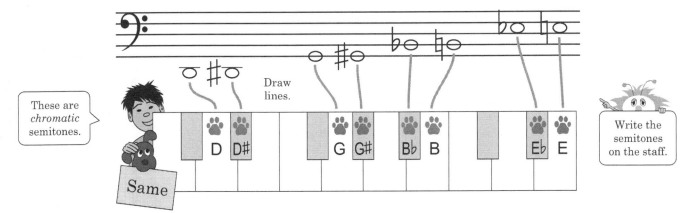

These are *chromatic* semitones.

Draw lines.

Same

Write the semitones on the staff.

C and C# make a *chromatic* semitone, because they are both named with the *same* alphabet letter. C and C# are a __chromatic__ semitone.

# Or Diatonic?

These are *diatonic* semitones.

This time, use two *different* letters to name each pair of notes.

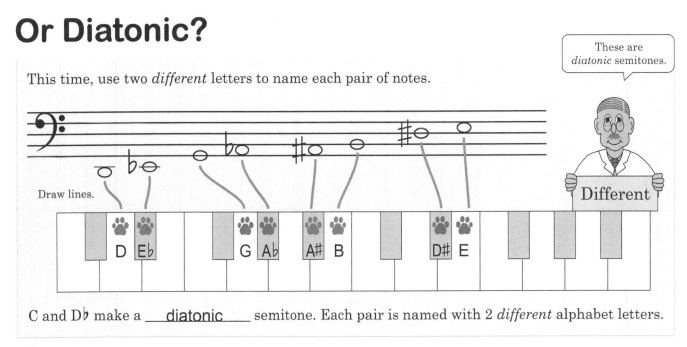

Draw lines.

Different

C and D♭ make a __diatonic__ semitone. Each pair is named with 2 *different* alphabet letters.

Next, look below the keyboard to see whether each semitone is diatonic or chromatic.
Name the paw print keys. Write the semitones on the staff.

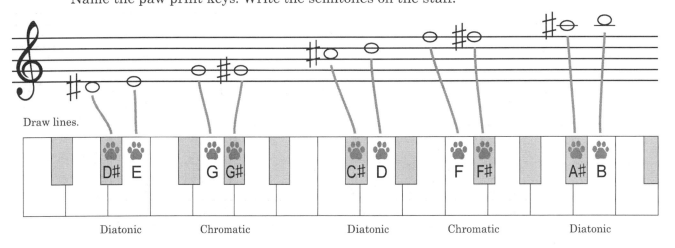

Draw lines.

Diatonic     Chromatic     Diatonic     Chromatic     Diatonic

Doctor Mozart Music Theory Workbook, Answers for Level 2 & 3.  © MMVIII, MMXV Machiko and Paul Christopher Musgrave.     Published by April Avenue Music.     www.DoctorMozart.com

# CHROMATIC AND DIATONIC

After each printed note, write a note
that is a semitone *higher*.

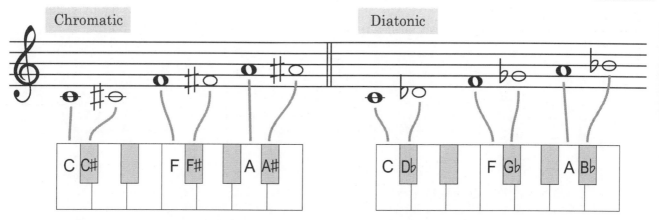

How to remember which is which: *Diatonic* and *Different* both start with **D**.

After each printed note, write a note that is a semitone *lower*. Draw lines. Name the notes.

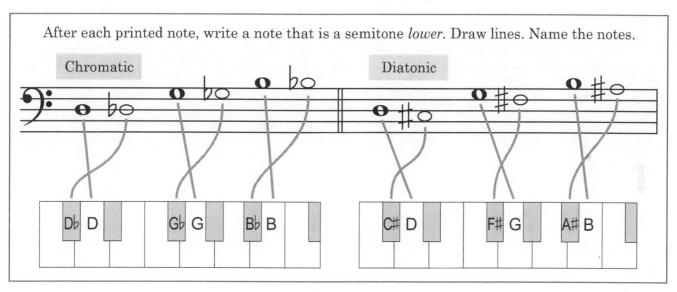

Look at the words below this keyboard. Name the paw print keys. Write the semitones on the staff.

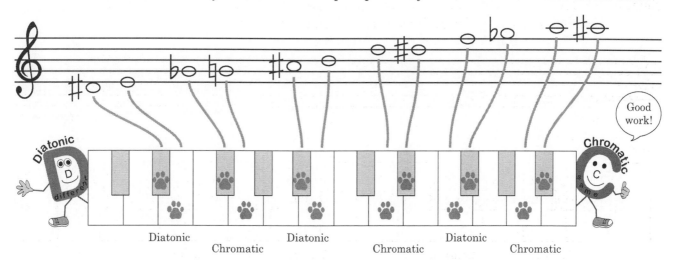

# ENHARMONIC Notes

Write each black key two different ways on the staff. Name the notes.

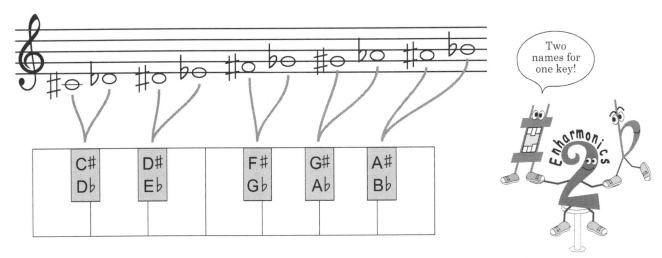

**Enharmonic equivalent** is another way of saying enharmonic note. D# and E♭ are enharmonic equivalents. C# and D♭ are also _____ **enharmonic** _____ **equivalents** _____.

For each *colored* paw print, write a chromatic semitone *up* on the staff. For each *white* paw print, write a chromatic semitone *down* on the staff. Draw lines from notes to keys.

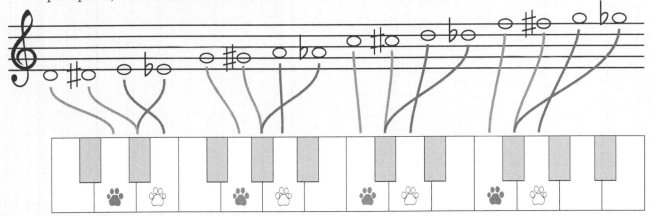

Write 5 pairs of enharmonic equivalent notes. Draw lines from notes to keys.

## This is just an example.

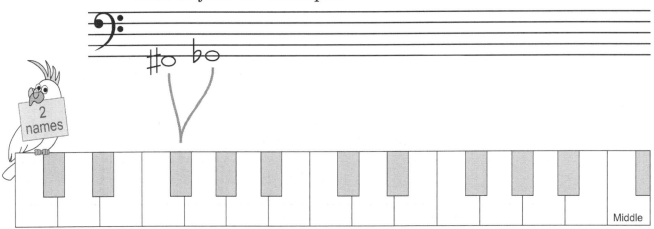

# 2 Half Steps = 1 Whole Step

Draw an arrow from each *left* paw print to the cat's face.
Then draw an arrow from each cat's face to the *right* paw
print. Mark each whole step with a square bracket.

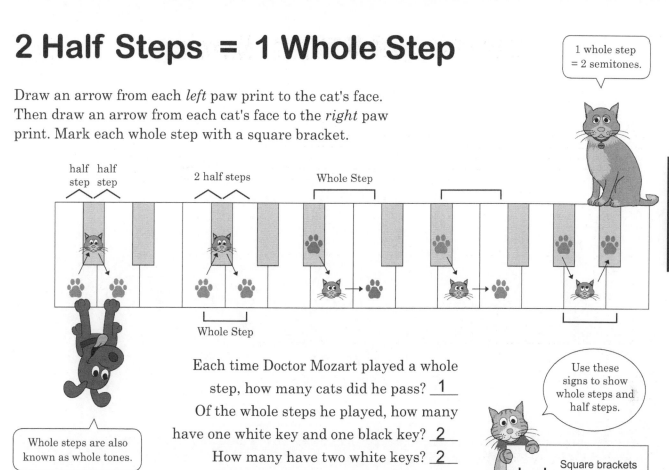

Each time Doctor Mozart played a whole
step, how many cats did he pass? __1__
Of the whole steps he played, how many
have one white key and one black key? __2__
How many have two white keys? __2__
How many have two black keys? __1__
One semitone = one ___half___ step.
One whole tone = one ___whole___ step.

Draw an arrow from each *left* paw print to the note
that is a whole step *higher*. Draw square brackets.

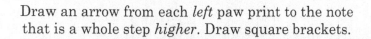

Next, draw an arrow from each *right* paw print to the
note that is a whole step *lower*. Draw square brackets.

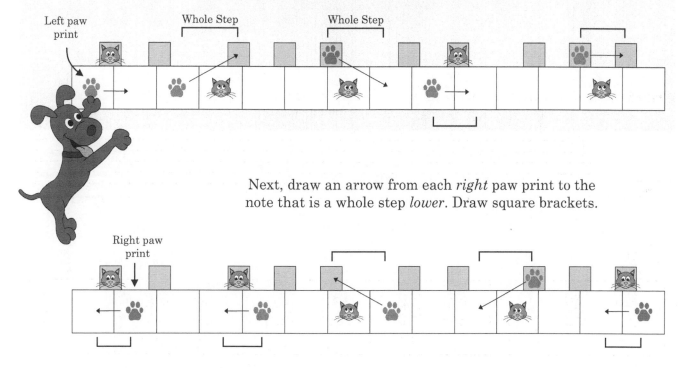

# Whole Steps Span Neighboring Letters

Circle all the pairs of letters that are right beside each other on the keyboard.

A (C D) (G A) (D E) G B D (G A) C (E F) (A B) (F G) D

The letters you circled are *neighboring* letters.

Always name whole steps with 2 *neighboring* letters.

For each paw print pair, name the white key first. Then use a *neighboring* letter to name the black key. Write each whole step on the staff.

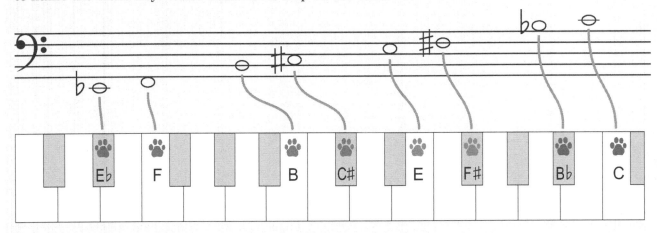

Whole steps made with 2 black keys can be named two ways. For each of these note pairs, write the whole step 2 different ways on the staff. Draw lines.

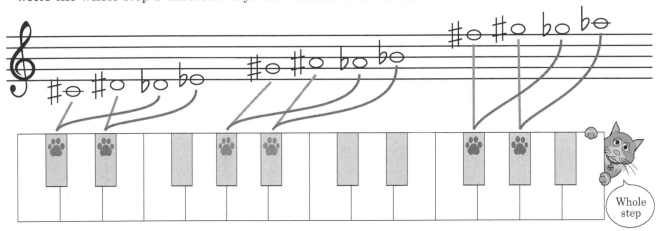

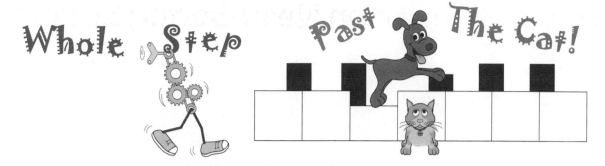

# Whole Step Past The Cat!

Write these whole steps on the staff. Use neighboring letters.

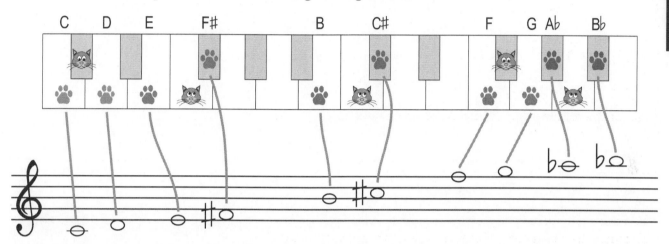

Doctor Mozart wants to play whole steps that span each cat. Name the notes he should play. Always use two *neighboring* letter names.

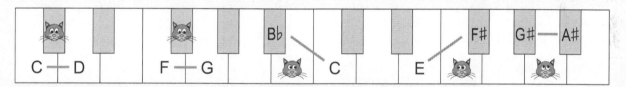

Above, how many whole steps have two white keys? __2__ How many have two black keys? __1__ How many have a white key and a black key? __2__

Circle any paw print pairs that make a whole step. Use neighboring letters to name them.

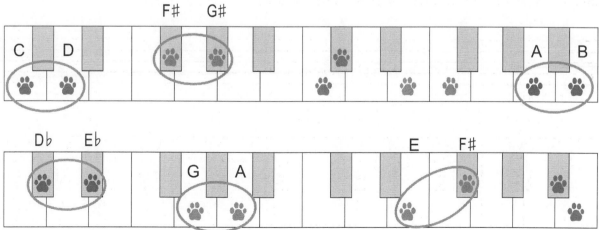

# Paw Print Practice

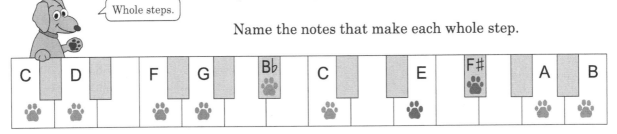

Name the notes that make each whole step.

Below, draw lines to match the meanings.

- Semitone
- Whole tone
- Whole step
- Half step
- The smallest distance between two keys on the keyboard
- A distance equal to two half steps

Name the whole steps. Write them on the staff.

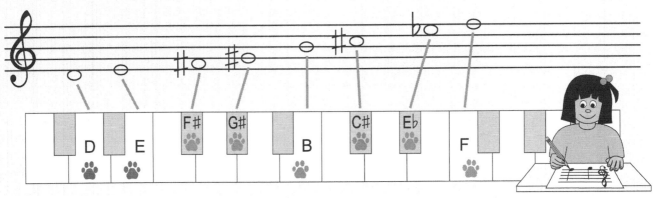

Put a check mark beside each answer that is true. Put an X beside any answer that is false.

A whole step can have

- Two white keys ✔
- Two black keys ✔
- A white key and a black key ✔

A half step can have

- Two white keys ✔
- Two black keys ✘
- A white key and a black key ✔

Write the whole steps and half steps on the staff. Draw square and V brackets.

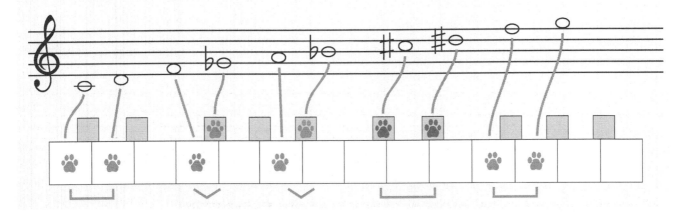

Doctor Mozart Music Theory Workbook, Answers for Level 2 & 3.  © MMVIII, MMXV Machiko and Paul Christopher Musgrave.   Published by April Avenue Music.   www.DoctorMozart.com

# Dots & Flags EXERCISE

Write one note in each box.

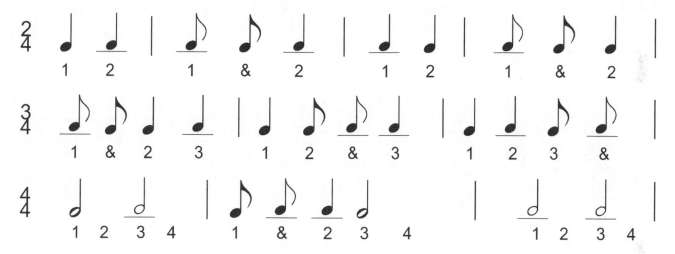

Write one note in each blank space. Number the beats. Tap and count.

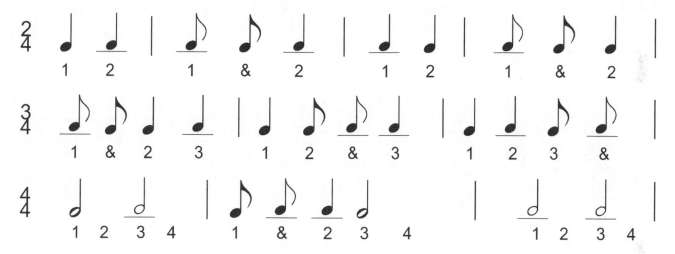

Each chocolate square equals one quarter note.
Write the *top* number for each time signature.

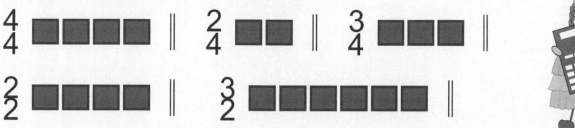

Write a treble clef and a time signature. Fill some bars with any notes you like. Number the beats.

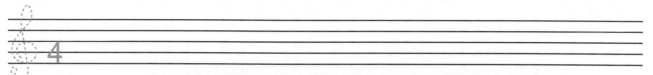

Teacher: The student must write a variety of notes,
adding to the correct number of beats in each bar.

Include some eighth notes, dotted half notes, staccato quarter notes, ledger notes, and accidentals.

# The C Major Scale

Trace the Roman numerals and the brackets. The Roman numerals are colored to show two *tetrachords*.

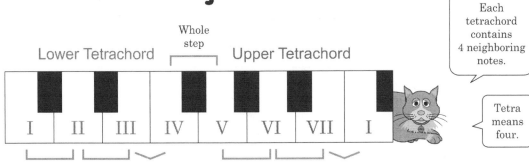

Each tetrachord contains 4 neighboring notes.

Tetra means four.

Each tetrachord contains __4__ neighboring notes.

Every **major scale** contains 2 tetrachords. Trace the brackets on this car.

Notice the __Whole__ step between the two tetrachords.

Next, draw square and V brackets.

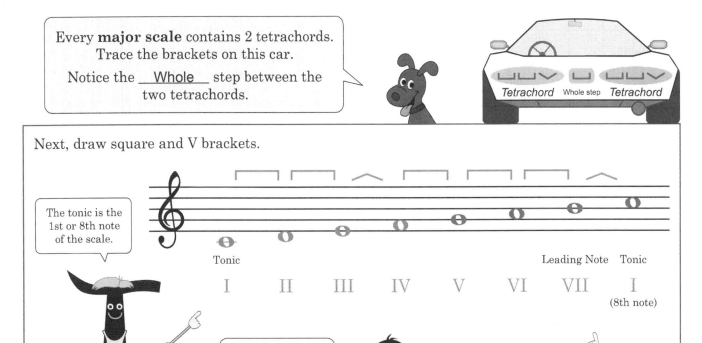

The tonic is the 1st or 8th note of the scale.

Tony

These 8 notes form a C Major scale. Trace the Roman numerals.

The leading note is the 7th note of the scale.

Larry

Tonic          Leading Note   Tonic

I    II    III    IV    V    VI    VII    I (8th note)

How many tetrachords are in this scale? __2__   How many notes are in each tetrachord? __4__

How many half steps are in each tetrachord? __1__

The first note of this scale is called the __tonic__. The seventh note is the __leading__ __note__.

The final note is the __tonic__ again. Between the two tetrachords, there is a __whole__ step.

Draw square and V brackets below this scale. Trace each T and L (for Tonic and Leading note).

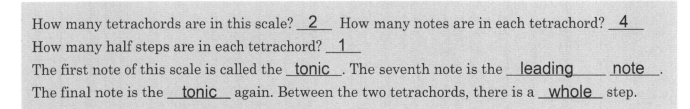

Ascending (going up)          Descending (going down)

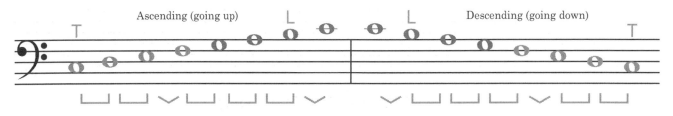

Doctor Mozart Music Theory Workbook, Answers for Level 2 & 3.   © MMVIII, MMXV  Machiko and Paul Christopher Musgrave.   Published by April Avenue Music.   www.DoctorMozart.com

# The G Major Scale

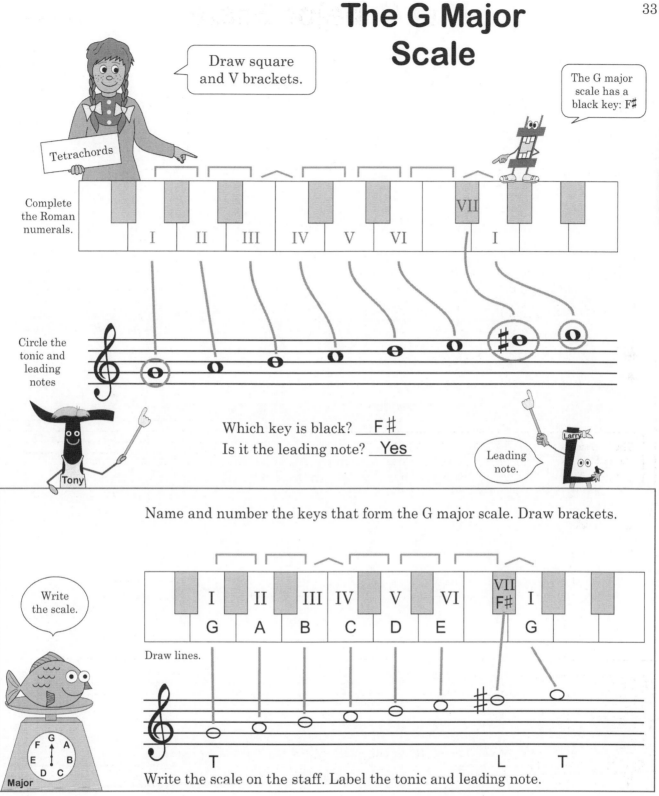

Draw square and V brackets.

The G major scale has a black key: F♯

2 A

Tetrachords

Complete the Roman numerals.

I   II   III   IV   V   VI   VII   I

Circle the tonic and leading notes

Which key is black? __F♯__
Is it the leading note? __Yes__

Leading note.

Name and number the keys that form the G major scale. Draw brackets.

Write the scale.

I   II   III   IV   V   VI   VII F♯   I
G   A   B   C   D   E   G

Draw lines.

T   L   T

Write the scale on the staff. Label the tonic and leading note.

Next, write the G major key signature. Write a G major scale, ascending and descending.

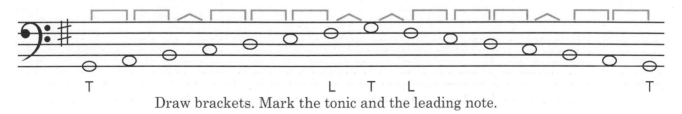

T   L   T   L   T

Draw brackets. Mark the tonic and the leading note.

Doctor Mozart Music Theory Workbook, Answers for Level 2 & 3.   © MMVIII, MMXV  Machiko and Paul Christopher Musgrave.   Published by April Avenue Music.   www.DoctorMozart.com

# The F Major Scale

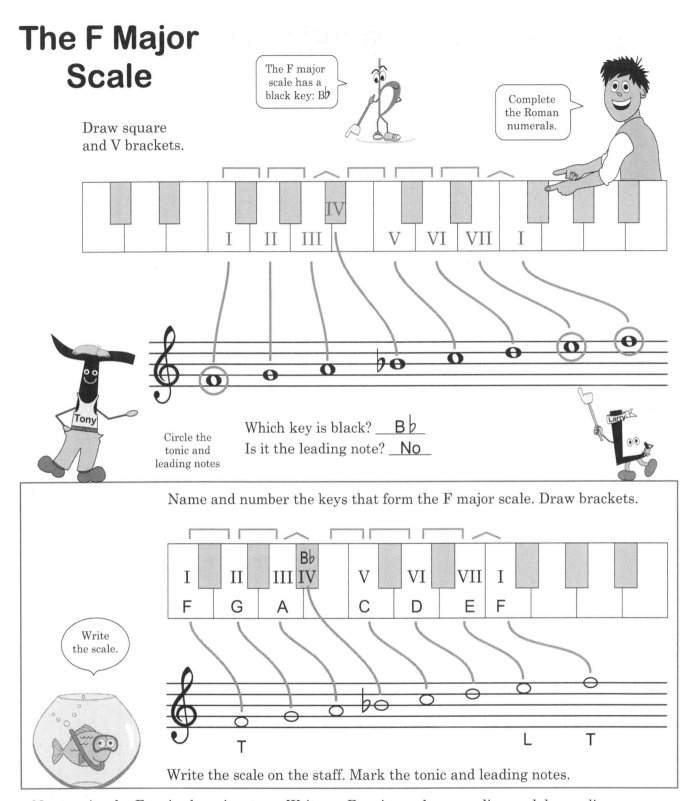

Draw square and V brackets.

The F major scale has a black key: B♭

Complete the Roman numerals.

Circle the tonic and leading notes

Which key is black? __B♭__
Is it the leading note? __No__

Name and number the keys that form the F major scale. Draw brackets.

Write the scale.

Write the scale on the staff. Mark the tonic and leading notes.

Next, write the F major key signature. Write an F major scale, ascending and descending.

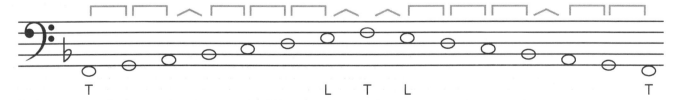

Draw brackets. Mark the tonic and leading notes.

Doctor Mozart Music Theory Workbook, Answers for Level 2 & 3. © MMVIII, MMXV Machiko and Paul Christopher Musgrave.    Published by April Avenue Music.    www.DoctorMozart.com

Trace and name each note.

Connect the notes that have the same name.

A  A  B  B  D  D  E  E

Draw lines.

2
A

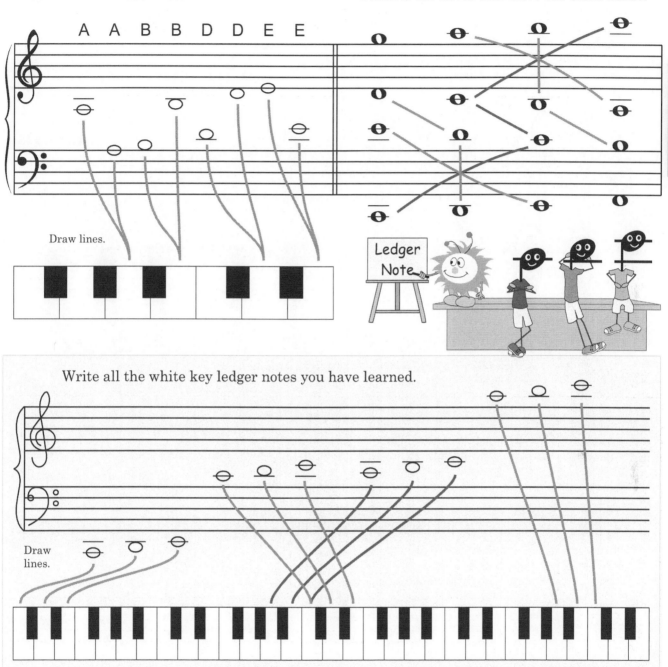

Ledger Note

Write all the white key ledger notes you have learned.

Draw lines.

Make a grand staff. For each letter, write a note near middle C – two different ways.

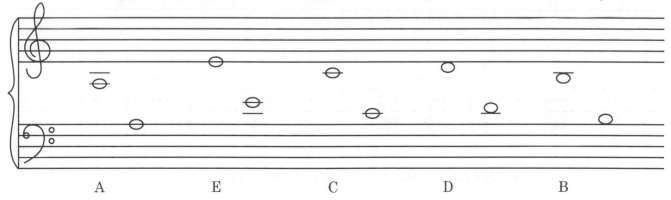

A          E          C          D          B

Doctor Mozart Music Theory Workbook, Answers for Level 2 & 3.   © MMVIII, MMXV  Machiko and Paul Christopher Musgrave.   Published by April Avenue Music.   www.DoctorMozart.com

# HaLF Step WHoLe Step Quiz

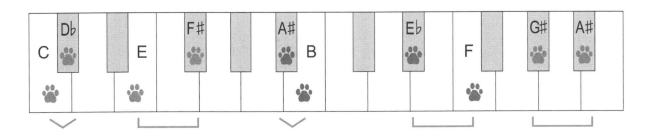

Name the whole steps and half steps.
Write square and V brackets.

Find a *half* step *above* each paw print, and mark that note with a letter H – for *h*alf step.
Find a *whole* step *above* each paw print, and mark that note with a letter W – for *w*hole step.

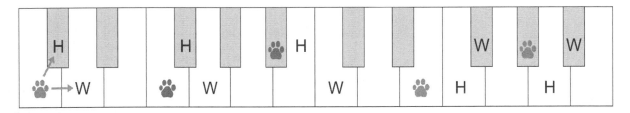

Find a *half* step *below* each paw print, and mark that note with a letter H.
Find a *whole* step *below* each paw print, and mark that note with a letter W.

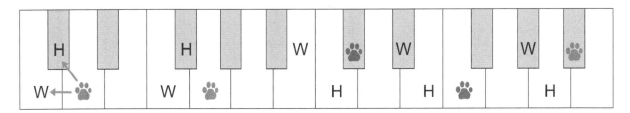

Mark each half step with a V bracket. Mark each whole step with a square bracket.

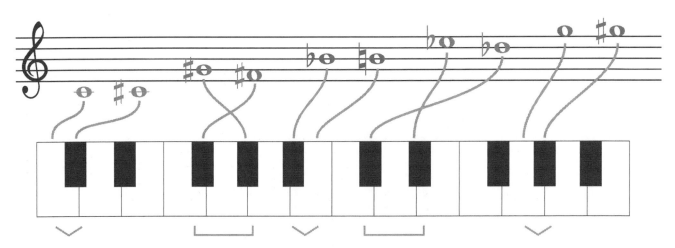

Doctor Mozart Music Theory Workbook, Answers for Level 2 & 3. © MMVIII, MMXV Machiko and Paul Christopher Musgrave.   Published by April Avenue Music.   www.DoctorMozart.com

Write one
note in each
empty space.

♩ + ♩. = ▬

♩. = ♩ + ▬

♪ + ♪ + 𝄾 + ♩ = ♩.

𝅝 = ♪ + ♪ + 𝄾 + ♩

Write a G major scale ascending and descending. Draw brackets. Mark the tonic and leading notes.

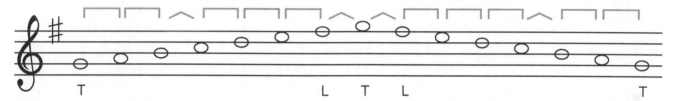

T       L   T   L                T

Write an F major scale going up and down. Draw brackets. Mark the tonic and leading notes.

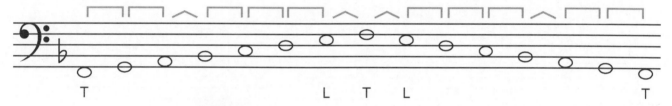

T       L   T   L                T

Tetrachords

Write an *eighth note* or a *quarter rest* or a *half rest* in each box. Number the beats.

$\frac{2}{4}$  1  2  | 1  &  2  | 1  2  | 1  &  2  |

$\frac{2}{2}$  1  &  2  | 1  &  2  &

$\frac{4}{4}$  1  2  3  4  | 1  2  3  4  | 1  &  2  3  4

Doctor Mozart Music Theory Workbook, Answers for Level 2 & 3.  © MMVIII, MMXV  Machiko and Paul Christopher Musgrave.  Published by April Avenue Music.  www.DoctorMozart.com

# EXPERT Review

Write the correct clef on each staff to make
semitones that contain only white keys.

Which clef?

Look at the words below this keyboard. Name the semitones. Write them on the staff.

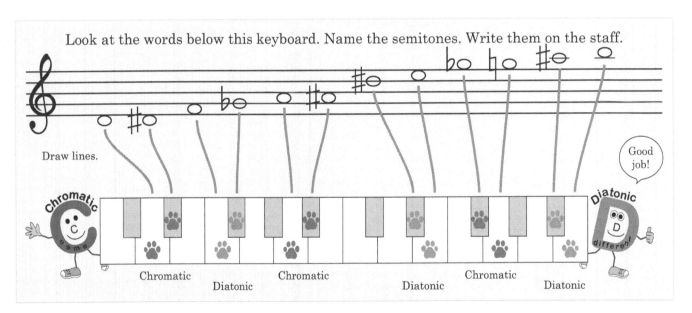

Draw lines.

Good job!

Chromatic  C  same

Diatonic  D  different

Chromatic

Diatonic

Chromatic

Diatonic

Chromatic

Diatonic

Make a grand staff and time signature. Fill some bars with notes. Number the beats.

Teacher: The student should use a variety of notes, as indicated below.
The time values should add up correctly to complete each bar.

Include quarter and half rests, eighth notes, dotted half notes, ledger notes, accidentals,
enharmonic equivalents, dynamics marks, and diatonic and chromatic semitones.

# Doctor Mozart® Music Theory Workbook

## In-Depth Piano Theory Fun for Children's Music Lessons and Home Schooling

### Level 2B - Partial Contents

Every day, start by reviewing what you learned the day before. Then complete just one or two exercises, or even a full page. Do this daily and you will make good progress.

2B

Highly Effective for Beginners Learning a Musical Instrument.

Doctor Mozart workbooks are filled with friendly cartoon characters. They make it fun to learn music theory in-depth. And in-depth music theory knowledge is essential for children learning a musical instrument. Use Doctor Mozart workbooks by themselves or with other teaching materials. Use them for music lessons and for home schooling.

The authors, Machiko and Paul Musgrave, are both graduates of Juilliard. Machiko has taught piano and theory at Soai University in Japan. Paul is an Associate of the Royal Conservatory of Music. The authors hope you enjoy using this book!

**Copyright laws protect the right of authors and publishers to earn a living from their work. Please respect these laws, and pay for the books you use and enjoy. Photocopying or reproducing this book in any manner may lead to prosecution.**

Many thanks to Kevin Musgrave for his meticulous proof-reading and insightful suggestions.

Created by Machiko and Paul Christopher Musgrave. Illustrated by Machiko Yamane Musgrave.            1.0.5

Doctor Mozart Music Theory Workbook, Answers for Level 2 & 3.   © MMVIII, MMXV  Machiko and Paul Christopher Musgrave.    Published by April Avenue Music.    www.DoctorMozart.com

# Where Should You Go Next?

Here are some signs that can help you find your way when reading music.

## D.C. al fine

D.C. = Da capo.
Capo means head.

When you see *D.C. al fine*, return to the beginning of the music. End at the word *fine*.

Da capo is pronounced duh KUH-po

Beginning

D.C. al fine

fine

*Fine* is pronounced FEE-ne.

Write *fine* below the staff, at the double bar line.

Trace the signs.

*Da capo al fine* means __return__ to the __beginning__ of the music. End at the word __fine__.

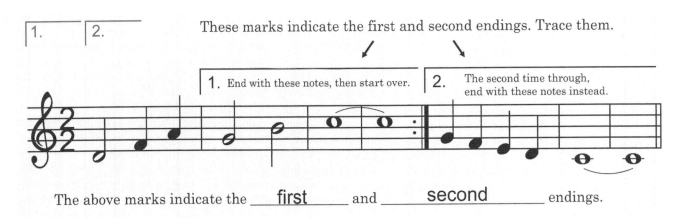

1.    2.

These marks indicate the first and second endings. Trace them.

1. End with these notes, then start over.

2. The second time through, end with these notes instead.

The above marks indicate the __first__ and __second__ endings.

## D.S.

D.S. = Dal segno (dal SAY-nyo).
Segno means *sign*.

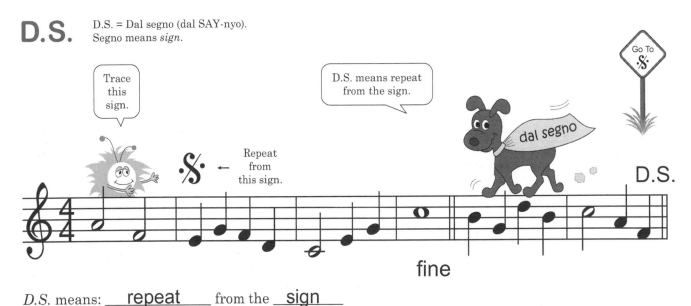

Go To

Trace this sign.

D.S. means repeat from the sign.

dal segno

D.S.

Repeat from this sign.

fine

*D.S.* means: __repeat__ from the __sign__

Doctor Mozart Music Theory Workbook, Answers for Level 2 & 3.  © MMVIII, MMXV  Machiko and Paul Christopher Musgrave.    Published by April Avenue Music.    www.DoctorMozart.com

# Step Over the Cat?

Review from Level 2A

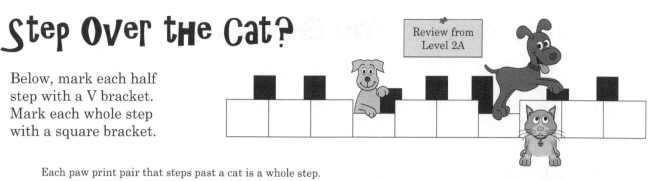

Below, mark each half step with a V bracket. Mark each whole step with a square bracket.

Each paw print pair that steps past a cat is a whole step.

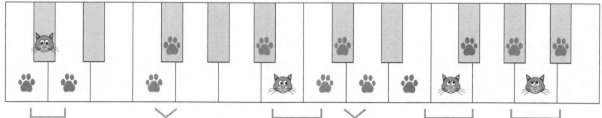

Find a *half* step *above* each paw print, and mark that note with a letter H – for half step.
Find a *whole* step *above* each paw print, and mark that note with a letter W – for whole step.

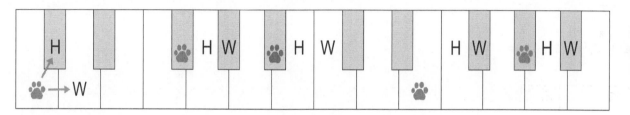

**2 B**

Find a *half* step *below* each paw print, and mark that note with a letter H.
Find a *whole* step *below* each paw print, and mark that note with a letter W.

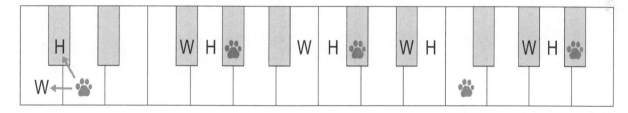

Draw lines from notes to keys. Mark each half step with a V bracket. Mark each whole step with a square bracket. Remember, bar lines cancel accidentals.

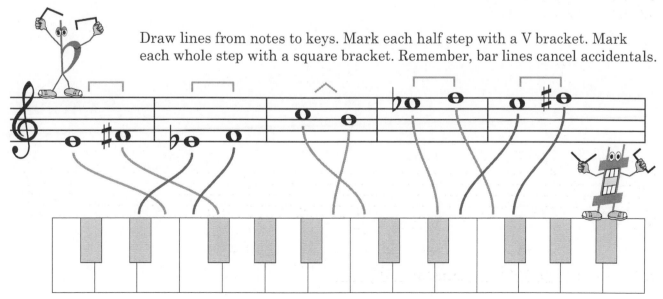

Doctor Mozart Music Theory Workbook, Answers for Level 2 & 3.   © MMVIII, MMXV  Machiko and Paul Christopher Musgrave.   Published by April Avenue Music.   www.DoctorMozart.com

# White Key Sharps and Flats

Trace the letters

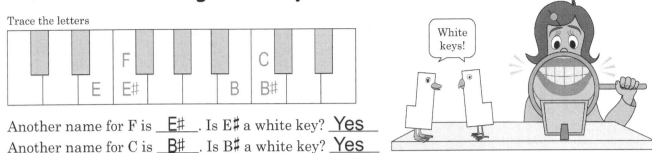

Another name for F is __E♯__ . Is E♯ a white key? __Yes__
Another name for C is __B♯__ . Is B♯ a white key? __Yes__

Below, label each E♯ and B♯ on the keyboard. Write the notes on the staff. Draw lines.

Middle | E♯ | B♯ | E♯ | B♯

Trace the letters

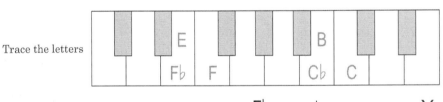

Another name for E is __F♭__ . Is F♭ a white key? __Yes__
Another name for B is __C♭__ . Is C♭ a white key? __Yes__

Below, label each F♭ and C♭ on the keyboard. Write the notes on the staff. Draw lines.

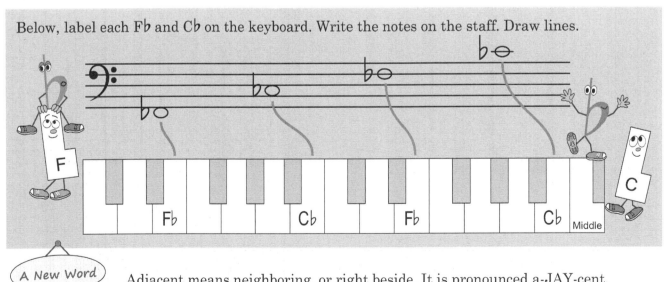

F♭ | C♭ | F♭ | C♭ | Middle

A New Word

Adjacent means neighboring, or right beside. It is pronounced a-JAY-cent.
Another word for neighboring is _____adjacent_____ . We will use this word often.

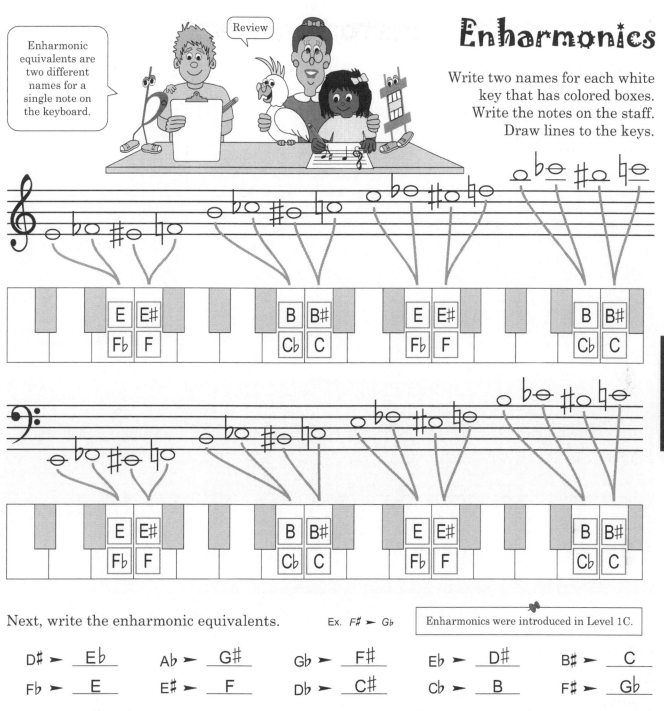

# Enharmonics

Enharmonic equivalents are two different names for a single note on the keyboard.

Write two names for each white key that has colored boxes. Write the notes on the staff. Draw lines to the keys.

2 B

Next, write the enharmonic equivalents.          Ex. *F♯* ➤ *G♭*          Enharmonics were introduced in Level 1C.

D♯ ➤ __E♭__          A♭ ➤ __G♯__          G♭ ➤ __F♯__          E♭ ➤ __D♯__          B♯ ➤ __C__

F♭ ➤ __E__          E♯ ➤ __F__          D♭ ➤ __C♯__          C♭ ➤ __B__          F♯ ➤ __G♭__

Below, for each white key that has two names, write both names on the keyboard and on the staff. Draw lines.

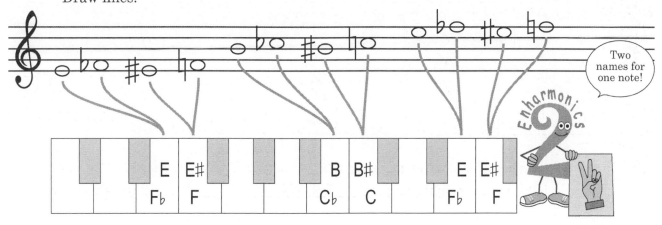

Two names for one note!

# Whole & Half Step Test

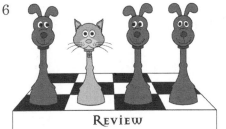

Chromatic half steps are written with just *one* letter name.

Diatonic half steps are written with __2__ adjacent letter names. Draw lines from notes to keys. Write CH above every chromatic half step. Write DH above every diatonic half step.

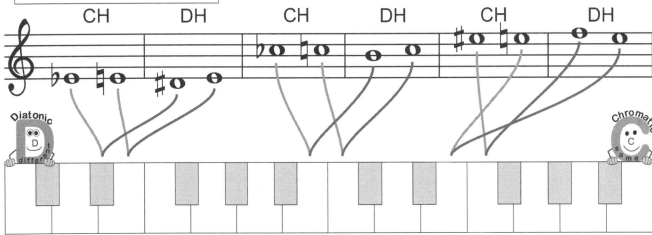

Remember, bar lines cancel accidentals.

Next, trace the clef. Write these whole steps two different ways on the bass staff. Draw lines.

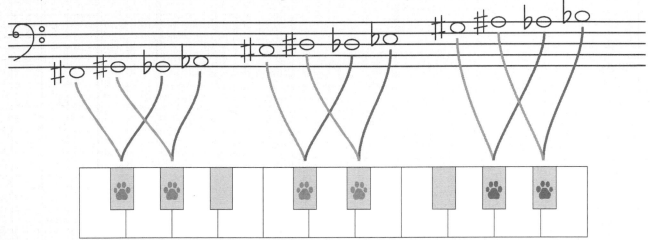

Trace the clef. Beside each note, write its enharmonic equivalent. Draw lines to the keyboard.

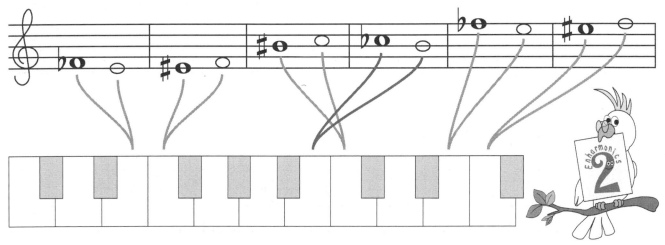

# Enharmonic Whole Steps

Name these whole steps two different ways on the keyboard, and on the staff. Follow the direction of the arrows.

I am D# and E♭!

Use enharmonic notes

D  E

Use adjacent letters.

2 B

Whole steps only!

Write the enharmonic equivalent of each note. Draw lines from the notes to the keyboard.

# A Major 2nd is a Whole Step.

One major 2nd
= 1 whole step

C   D

A major 2nd spans 2 alphabet letters.
M2 is the symbol for major 2nd.

Step past me
if you want
a major 2nd.

M2 means
major 2nd.

Name each
M2 with 2
adjacent
letters.

Under each major 2nd, draw a square bracket
and write M2. Name the paw print keys.

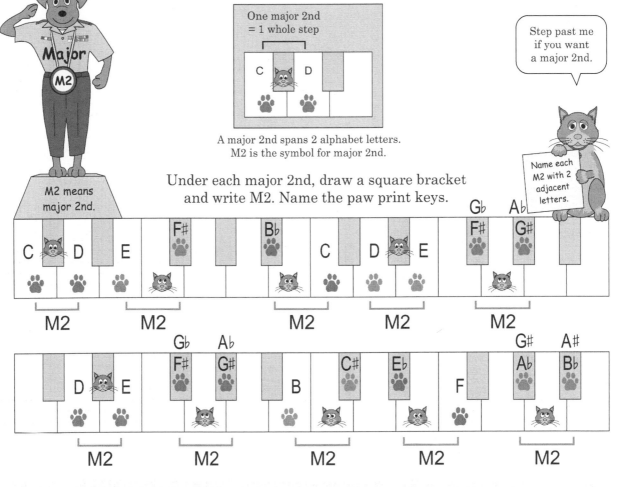

How many of the major 2nds above contain 2 black keys? ____3____

How many span 2 white keys? __3__ How many include a black key and a white key? __4__

**1 whole step = 1 whole tone = 1 major 2nd = 1 M2.**

1 whole step = 1 whole **tone** = 1 **major** 2nd = 1 M **2** .

Next, write these major 2nds on the staff. Follow the direction of the arrows.
Use adjacent letters. Draw lines.

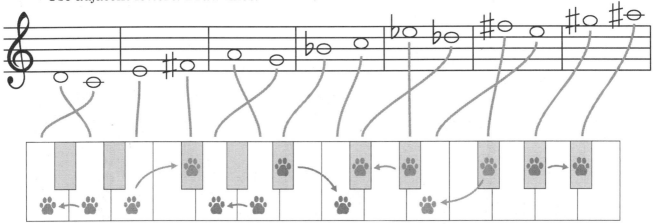

# Major 2nd Quiz

Write each major 2nd on the staff.
Follow the direction of the arrows.
Use adjacent letters. Draw lines.

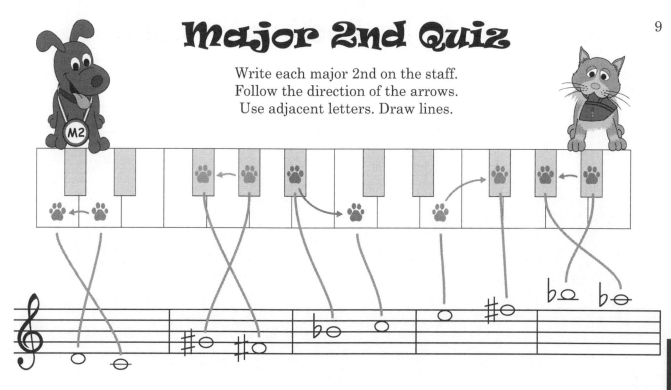

After each note, write a major 2nd. Follow the direction of the arrows.

**2 B**

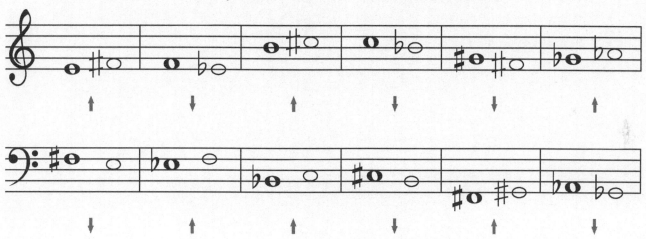

Below, write some major 2nds. Make some go up, and others go down. Include some black keys and ledger notes. Draw lines from notes to keys.

This is just an example answer.

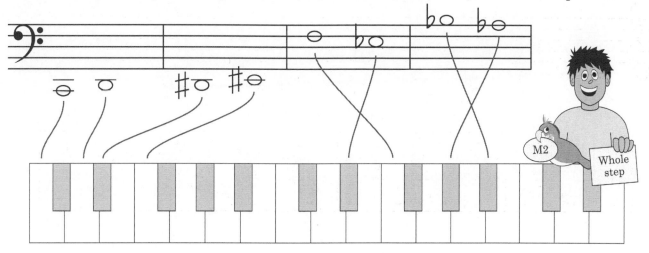

Whole step

Doctor Mozart Music Theory Workbook, Answers for Level 2 & 3. © MMVIII, MMXV Machiko and Paul Christopher Musgrave. Published by April Avenue Music. www.DoctorMozart.com

# How to Measure Intervals

An interval is the distance between two notes. A major 2nd is a kind of ___interval___.

An interval is the distance between two ___notes___.

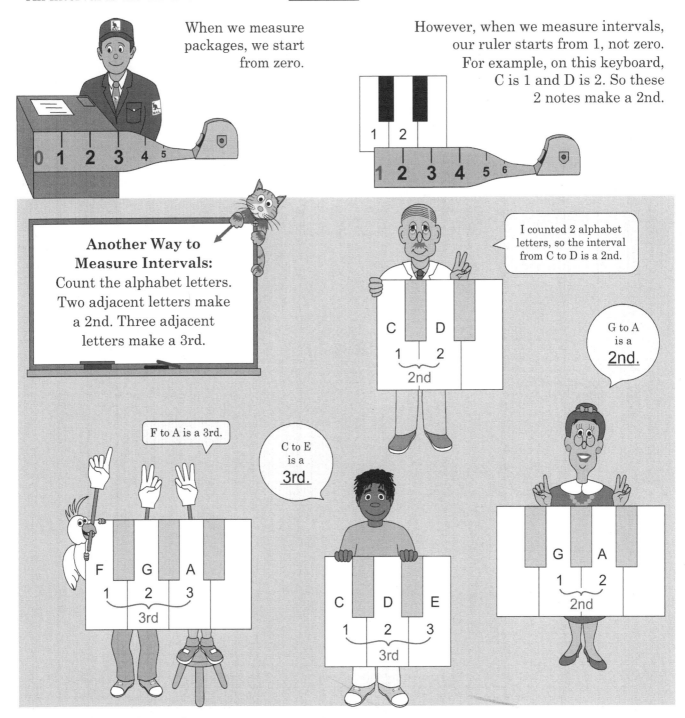

Number the keys spanned by each bracket. Name the intervals.

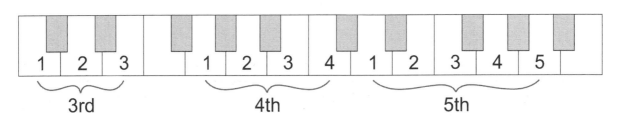

# A Minor 2nd is Smaller

One minor 2nd = one half step

A minor 2nd spans 2 alphabet letters

Trace the brackets at left. Is a *minor 2nd* smaller than a major 2nd? __Yes__
One diatonic half step = one ___minor___ 2nd = one m2.

Below, label each minor 2nd with m2 and a V bracket. Label each major 2nd with M2 and a square bracket. Name the paw print keys. Use adjacent alphabet letters.

A minor 2nd is a diatonic half step.

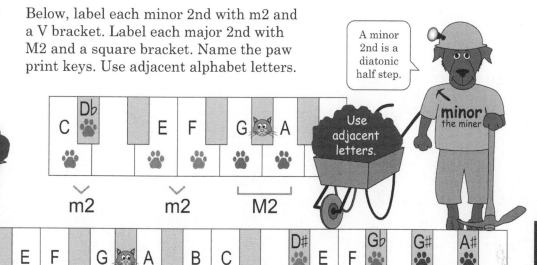

m2 is spelled with a lower case m.

m2

Use adjacent letters.

minor the miner

How many minor 2nds did you find above that contain 2 black keys? ___0___
How many span 2 white keys? __3__ How many include a black key and a white key? __4__
**1 diatonic half step = 1 diatonic semitone = 1 minor 2nd = 1 m2.**
1 diatonic half step = 1 diatonic ___semitone___ = 1 ___minor___ 2nd = 1 _m2_.

Next, write these minor 2nds on the staff. Use adjacent alphabet letters. Follow the direction of the arrows. Draw lines from notes to keys.

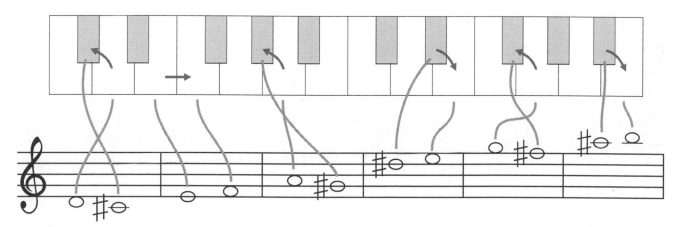

One minor 2nd = 1 ___diatonic___ semitone = one _m_ 2. Why is a *chromatic* semitone not a minor 2nd? Because its two notes are named with just one alphabet letter. Is the interval A to A♯ a minor 2nd? __No__. It is not a minor 2nd, because its notes are named with just one letter.

Doctor Mozart Music Theory Workbook, Answers for Level 2 & 3. © MMVIII, MMXV Machiko and Paul Christopher Musgrave. Published by April Avenue Music. www.DoctorMozart.com

# Adjacent Letters for Minor 2nds

Write a minor 2nd in each pair of boxes. Write the notes on the staff. Follow the direction of the arrows. Draw lines.

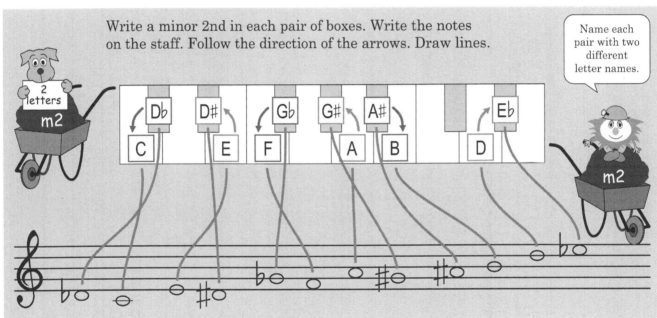

Below, name the notes. Draw lines. Write m2 above each minor 2nd. Write CH above each chromatic half step.

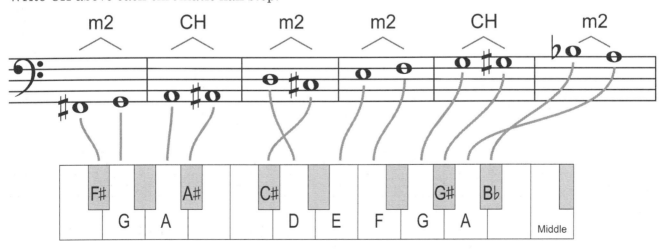

Doctor Mozart Music Theory Workbook, Answers for Level 2 & 3. © MMVIII, MMXV Machiko and Paul Christopher Musgrave. Published by April Avenue Music. www.DoctorMozart.com

# Major & Minor 2nd Quiz

Every 2nd is made with

two _____ **adjacent** _____
alphabet letters.

Below, at each major 2nd, circle
the Major's hat. At each minor 2nd,
circle the miner's hat.

Below, write three different minor 2nds, and three different major 2nds. Make some go up, and others go down. Use notes of various different lengths. Draw lines from notes to keys. At each 2nd, write M2 or m2. Draw square and V brackets.

Teacher: Check to ensure the student has followed the instructions. This exercise allows some creativity.

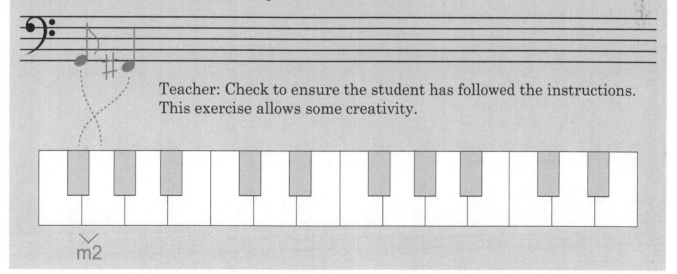

Next, write major and minor 2nds, as indicated by the hats and arrows.

# Time, Terms, & Enharmonics Review

Draw lines to match each term or sign with its meaning. Some lines may go to the same place.

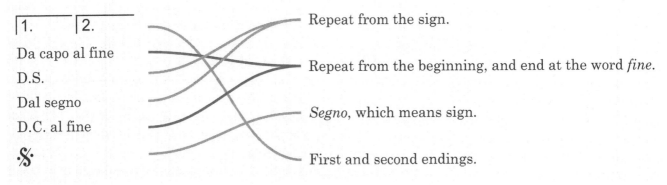

| 1. | 2. |
|----|----|

Da capo al fine

D.S.

Dal segno

D.C. al fine

𝄋

Repeat from the sign.

Repeat from the beginning, and end at the word *fine*.

*Segno*, which means sign.

First and second endings.

Draw lines to match each rest with a note of the same length.

Write the enharmonic equivalent of each note. Draw lines from the notes to the keyboard.

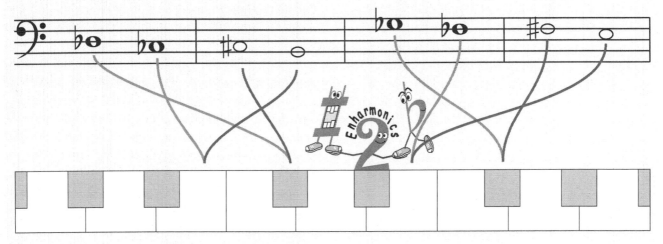

# Eighths at Rest

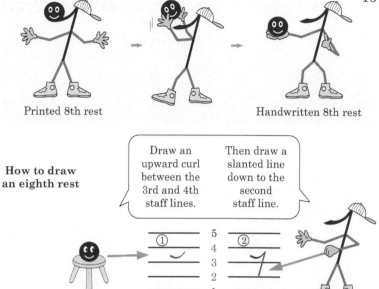

Printed 8th rest → Handwritten 8th rest

← This is an eighth rest. It means you should stay silent for the length of an eighth note.

**How to draw an eighth rest**

Draw an upward curl between the 3rd and 4th staff lines. Then draw a slanted line down to the second staff line.

Below, trace the eighth rests. Then draw 6 more.

Complete these sums.

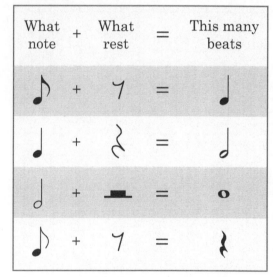

| What note | + | What rest | = | This many beats |
|---|---|---|---|---|
| ♪ | + | 𝄽 | = | ♩ |
| ♩ | + | 𝄾 | = | ♩ |
| ♩ | + | ▬ | = | 𝅝 |
| ♪ | + | 𝄽 | = | 𝄿 |

| This note | + | What short rest | + | What longer rest | = | This many beats |
|---|---|---|---|---|---|---|
| ♪ *quarter note* | + | 𝄽 | + | 𝄾 | = | ♩ |
| ♪ *quarter note* | + | 𝄽 | + | 𝄾 | = | ▬ |
| ♩ *half note* | + | 𝄾 | + | ▬ | = | ▬ |
| ♩ *half note* | + | 𝄾 | + | ▬ | = | 𝅝 |

Below, draw lines to match the rests, the notes, and the number of beats.

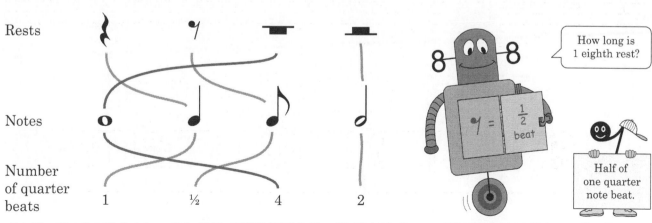

Rests

Notes

Number of quarter beats     1     ½     4     2

How long is 1 eighth rest?

𝄽 = ½ beat

Half of one quarter note beat.

Doctor Mozart Music Theory Workbook, Answers for Level 2 & 3.  © MMVIII, MMXV Machiko and Paul Christopher Musgrave.   Published by April Avenue Music.   www.DoctorMozart.com

# Pass 2 Cats for a Major 3rd

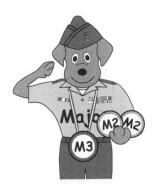

A major 3rd equals two major 2nds.

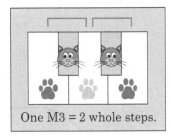

One M3 = 2 whole steps.

M3 is the symbol for major 3rd.
The upper case M means major.

Trace the gray brackets at left. Two major seconds together make a major 3rd, or M3.
A major 3rd equals two ___major___ 2nds.
A major 3rd also equals two ___whole___ steps.
To make a major 3rd, we pass __2__ cats.

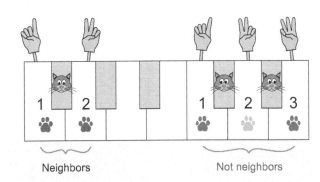

Neighbors          Not neighbors

What note is 2 whole steps above C? __E__.
C to E is a ___major___ 3rd, or M3.
The symbol for major 3rd is M_3_.

The 2 notes in a major 3rd are not neighbors. They span 3 alphabet letters.

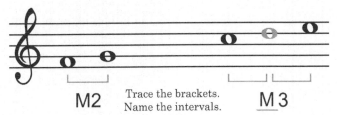

M2     Trace the brackets.     M3
       Name the intervals.

Below, number the bracketed keys. Name the intervals. Write them on the staff. Draw lines.

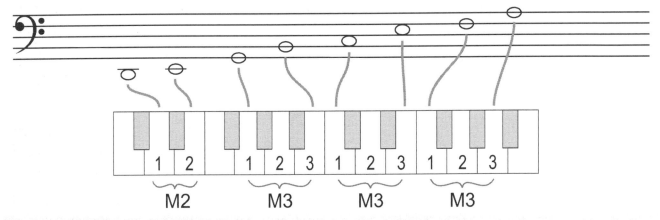

M2          M3          M3          M3

Write some major 3rds on the keyboard and on the staff. Draw lines and square brackets.

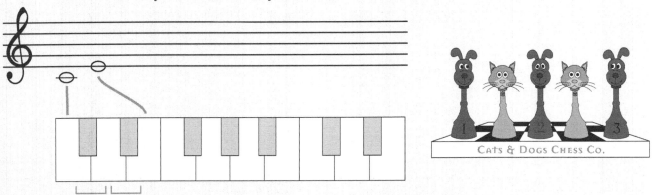

CATS & DOGS CHESS CO.

Doctor Mozart Music Theory Workbook, Answers for Level 2 & 3.  © MMVIII, MMXV  Machiko and Paul Christopher Musgrave.     Published by April Avenue Music.     www.DoctorMozart.com

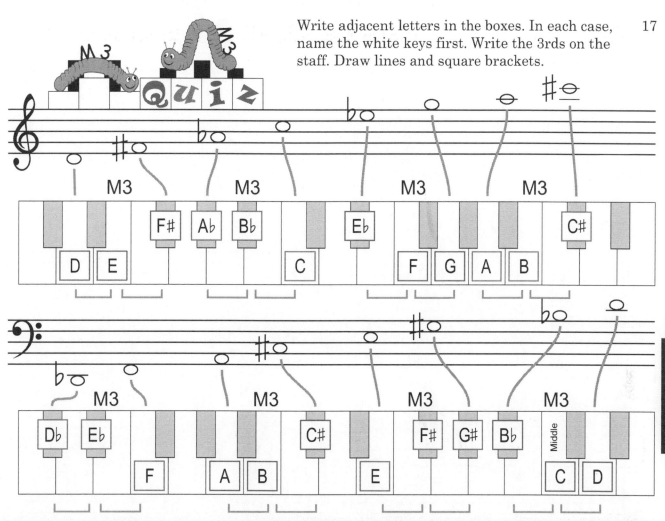

Above each paw print, write a major 3rd on the keyboard and the staff . Draw lines and brackets.

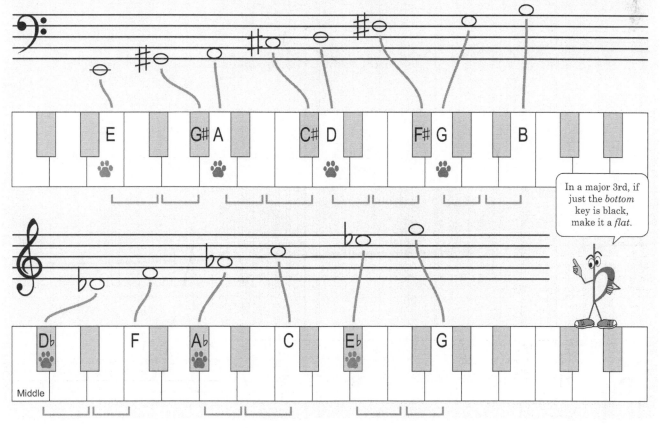

In a major 3rd, if just the *bottom* key is black, make it a *flat*.

2 B

# Major 3rds Up and Down

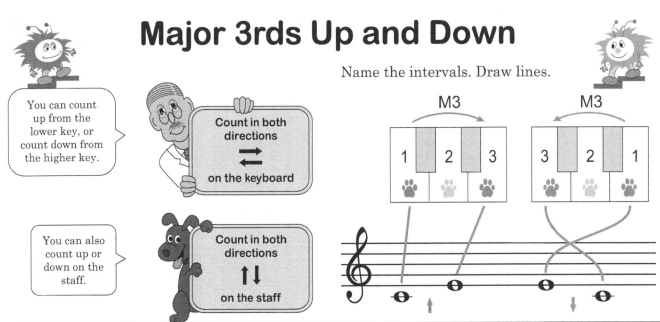

Name the intervals. Draw lines.

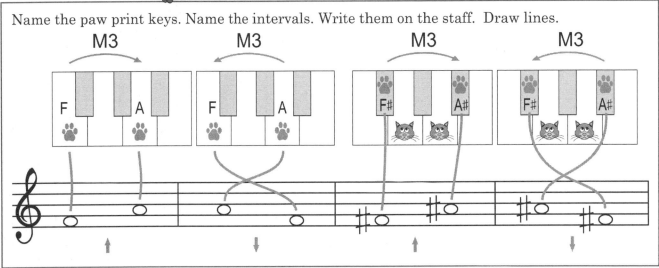

Name the paw print keys. Name the intervals. Write them on the staff. Draw lines.

Name the intervals. Write them on the staff. Follow the direction of the arrows. Draw lines.

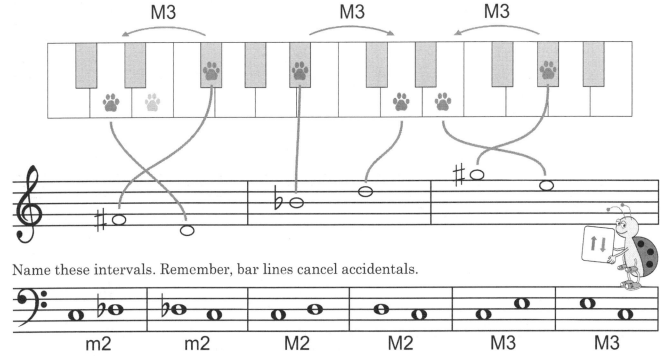

Name these intervals. Remember, bar lines cancel accidentals.

m2      m2      M2      M2      M3      M3

Doctor Mozart Music Theory Workbook, Answers for Level 2 & 3.  © MMVIII, MMXV  Machiko and Paul Christopher Musgrave.    Published by April Avenue Music.    www.DoctorMozart.com

# A Minor 3rd is Smaller

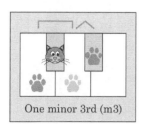

One minor 3rd (m3)

Trace the gray brackets at left.
1 minor 3rd equals
1 whole step + one __half__ step.

Below, write adjacent alphabet letters
in the boxes to show minor 3rds.
Draw square and V brackets.

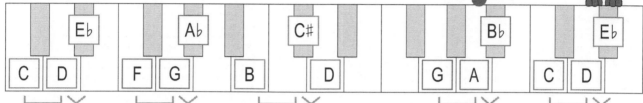

What note is 1 whole step + 1 half step above C? __E♭__. What note is 1 whole step + 1 half step above F? __A♭__. Each of these intervals is a minor 3rd, or m3. A minor 3rd is the same as one __whole__ step plus one __half__ step. It is the same as 1 M2 + 1 m__2__.

**2 B**

Below, draw square and V brackets to show the minor 3rds. Write the minor thirds on the staff. Draw lines from notes to keys.

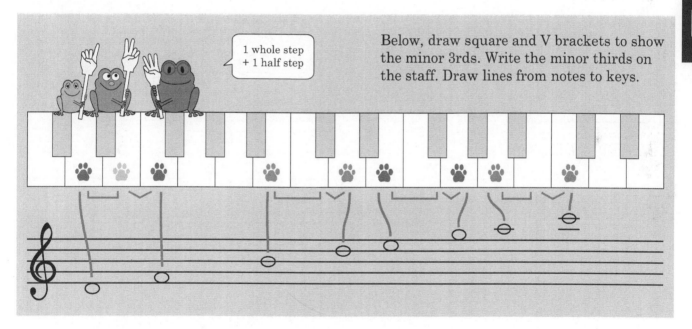

1 whole step + 1 half step

Next, write a minor 3rd above each given note on the staff.
Draw square and V brackets. Draw lines to the keyboard.

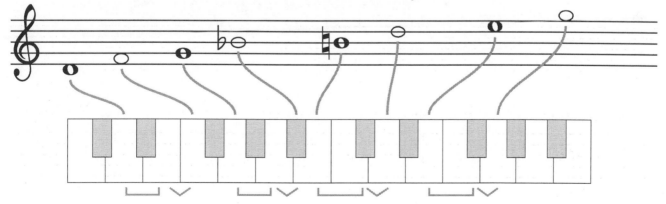

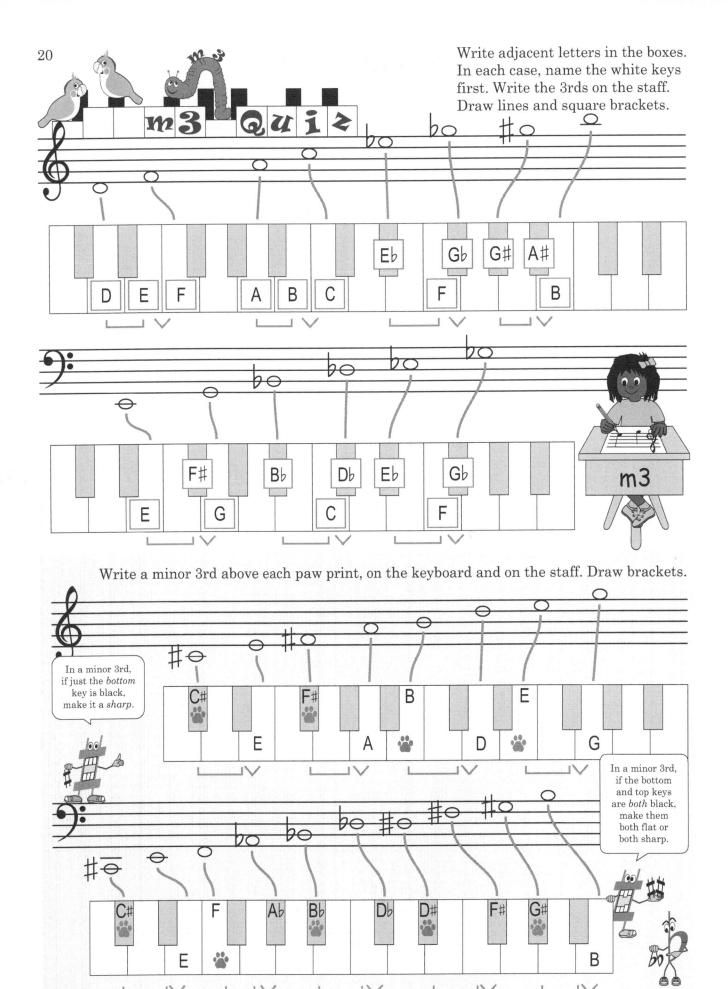

# M3 or m3?

Under each bracket, write M3 for major 3rd, or m3 for minor 3rd.

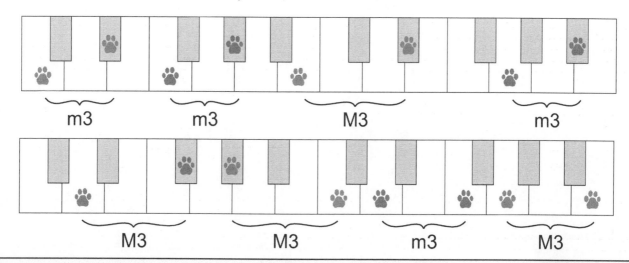

m3    m3    M3    m3

M3    M3    m3    M3

Under each pair of paw prints, draw square and V brackets. Write M3 or m3. Write the 3rds on the staff. Draw lines from notes to keys.

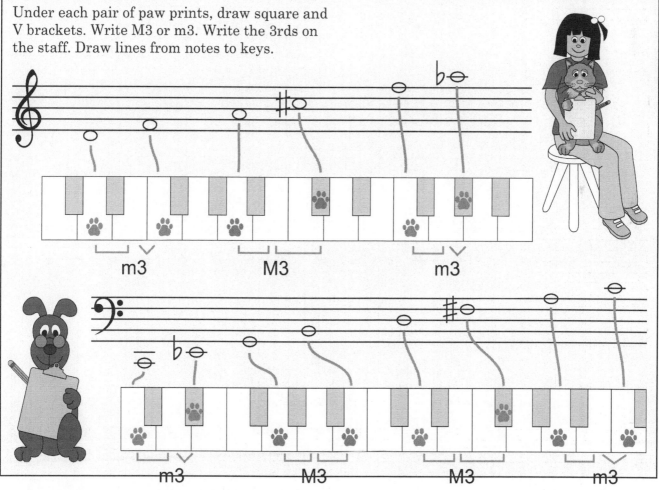

m3    M3    m3

m3    M3    M3    m3

Under each bracket, write M3 or m3.

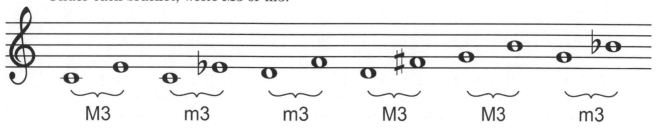

M3    m3    m3    M3    M3    m3

# Tapping Eighths

Tap this rhythm, hands together, while
counting the beats aloud. Repeat the
rhythm until you can tap it well.

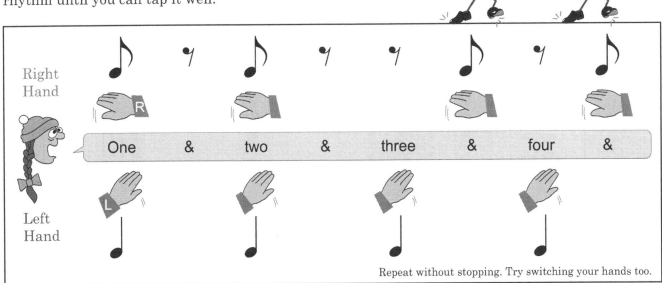

One & & two & three & four &

Right
Hand

Left
Hand

Repeat without stopping. Try switching your hands too.

If the bottom number in a time signature is 8, then each beat is one 8th note long.
Below, number the beats. Write any 8th rests needed to complete each bar.
Tap each rhythm, hands together, while counting aloud. Repeat until perfect.

Add rests. Tap and count.

Try switching your hands!

Doctor Mozart Music Theory Workbook, Answers for Level 2 & 3.   © MMVIII, MMXV  Machiko and Paul Christopher Musgrave.    Published by April Avenue Music.    www.DoctorMozart.com

# Measure Your Rests

Number the beats. Write an
ampersand (&) under any note or rest
that is between the beats. Draw the
bar lines. Tap while counting.

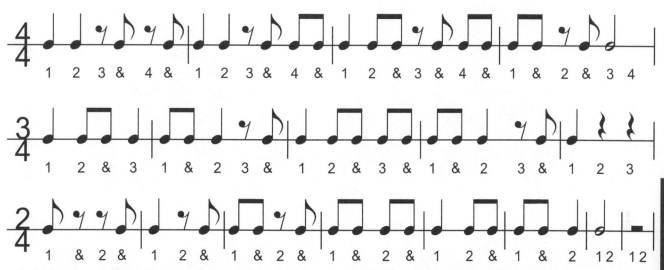

Write a single rest at each X. Number the beats.

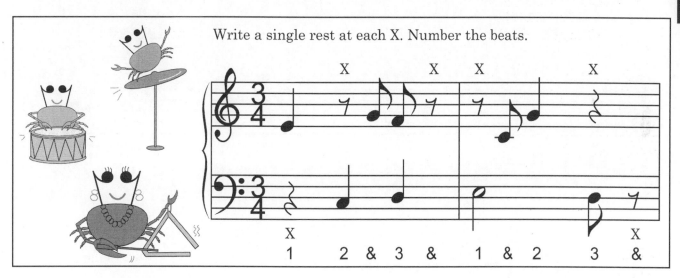

2 B

Next, make a grand staff and a 4/4 time signature. Write any half, quarter, and eighth notes
and rests you like. Include some ledger notes. Number the beats. Tap and count.

1

Doctor Mozart Music Theory Workbook, Answers for Level 2 & 3.   © MMVIII, MMXV  Machiko and Paul Christopher Musgrave.   Published by April Avenue Music.   www.DoctorMozart.com

# Convert Major 3rds to Minor 3rds

A major 3rd is made with two ___whole___ steps. A minor 3rd is made with one ___whole___ step and one ___half___ step. A ___major___ 3rd is larger than a ___minor___ 3rd. Can you convert a major 3rd into a minor 3rd? Yes you can! Just make the major 3rd one half step smaller. You can do that by lowering the top note.

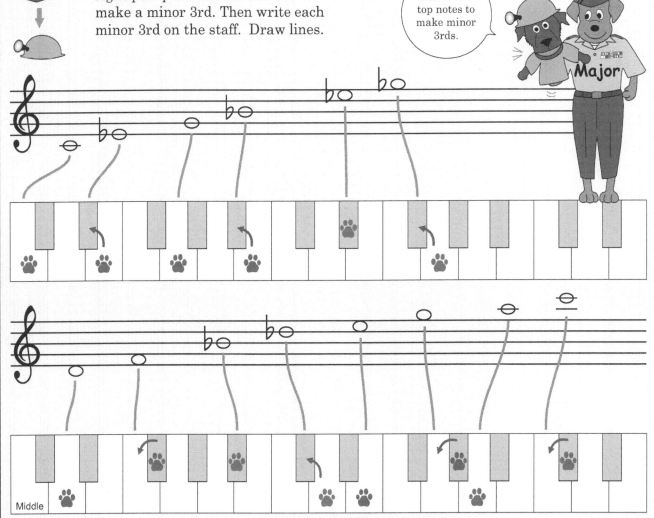

# Convert Minor 3rds to Major 3rds

You can convert a minor 3rd into a major 3rd. Just make the minor 3rd one half step larger. To do that, raise the top note.

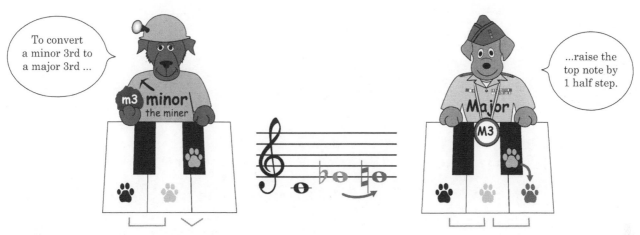

Draw red arrows to show how each right paw print should move to make a major 3rd. Then write each major 3rd on the staff.

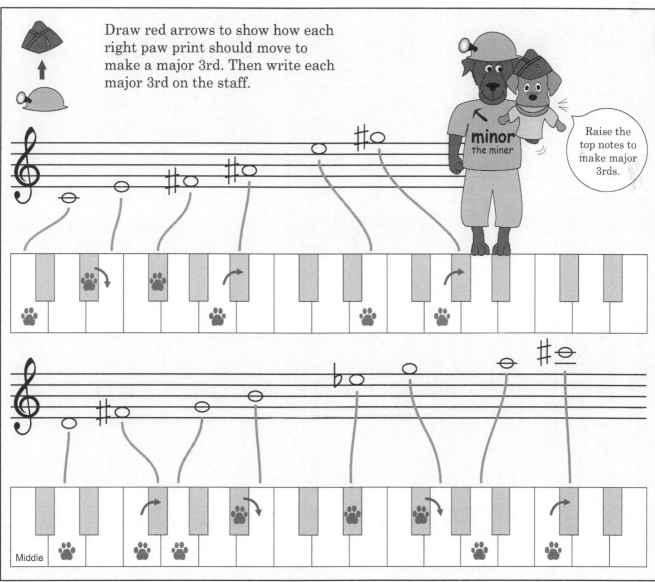

# 2 Ways to Make a Minor 3rd

A whole step
and a half step,

or a half step
and a whole step.

minor 3rd

You can make a minor 3rd by starting with a whole step – or by starting with a half step.
A whole step plus a half step gets you to the same place as a half step plus a whole step.

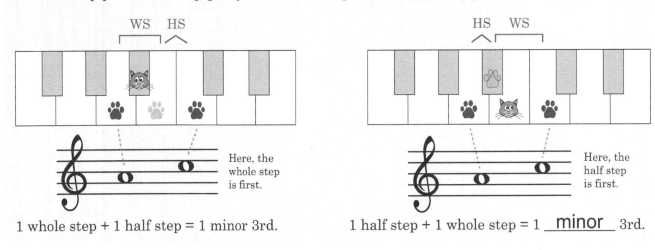

1 whole step + 1 half step = 1 minor 3rd.

1 half step + 1 whole step = 1 __minor__ 3rd.

In each colored box, count to a minor 3rd two different ways. Number the keys to show how.

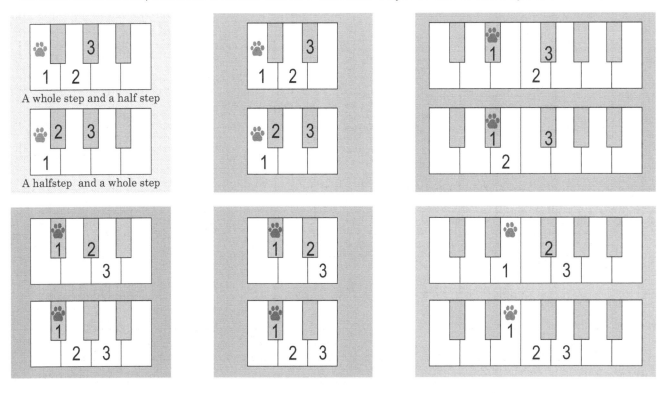

A whole step and a half step

A halfstep and a whole step

Doctor Mozart Music Theory Workbook, Answers for Level 2 & 3.  © MMVIII, MMXV  Machiko and Paul Christopher Musgrave.     Published by April Avenue Music.     www.DoctorMozart.com

# Major & Minor 3rd Quiz

Write the intervals indicated, up from each given note.
Draw lines to the keys. Name the keys.

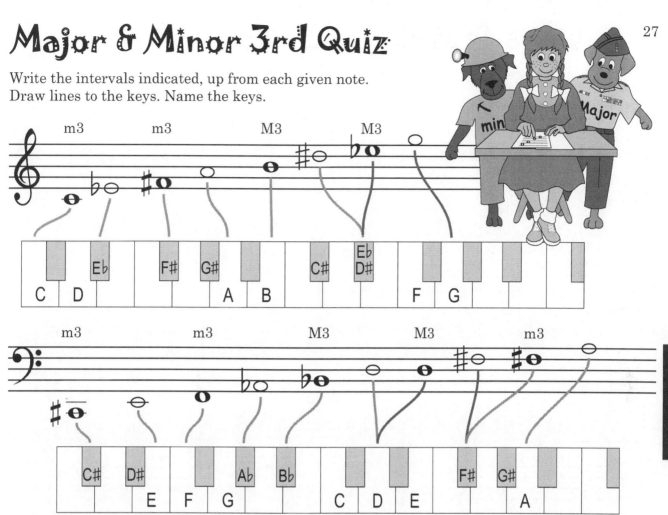

Number the lower keyboard so that the half step comes first in each m3. Draw brackets.

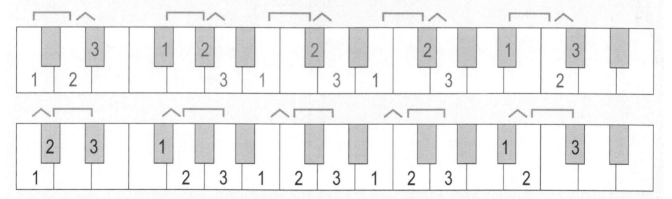

Below, make the minor 3rds major, and make the major 3rds minor. Draw lines to the keys.

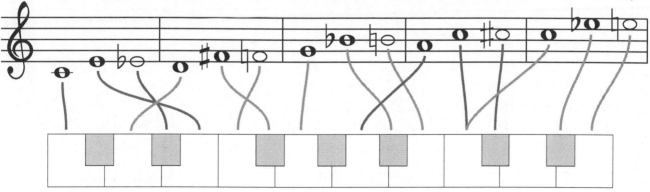

Doctor Mozart Music Theory Workbook, Answers for Level 2 & 3.   © MMVIII, MMXV Machiko and Paul Christopher Musgrave.   Published by April Avenue Music.   www.DoctorMozart.com

# Sharp or Flat?

If a 3rd contains a black key, is it easier to write it with a sharp or a flat? Look at this table to find out.

| Sharp or flat? How to decide. | If the **bottom** note is black: | If the **top** note is black: | If **both** notes are black: |
|---|---|---|---|
| **Major 3rd** | Make it ♭ | Make it ♯ | Make both ♯ or both ♭ |
| **Minor 3rd** | Make it ♯ | Make it ♭ | |

These are *not* rules. These are suggestions to help make writing 3rds *easy*.

Look at the hats. Then make a 3rd *above* each colored key as shown. Draw connecting arrows.

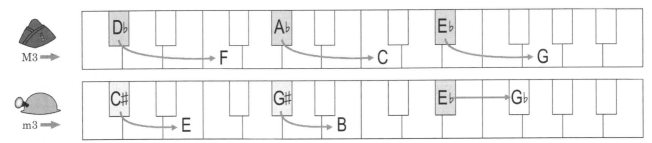

Look at the hats. Then make a 3rd *below* each colored key as shown. Draw connecting arrows.

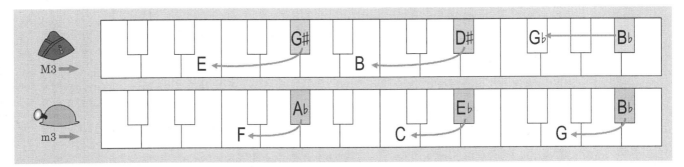

Name each interval. Draw lines to the keys. Remember, bar lines cancel accidentals.

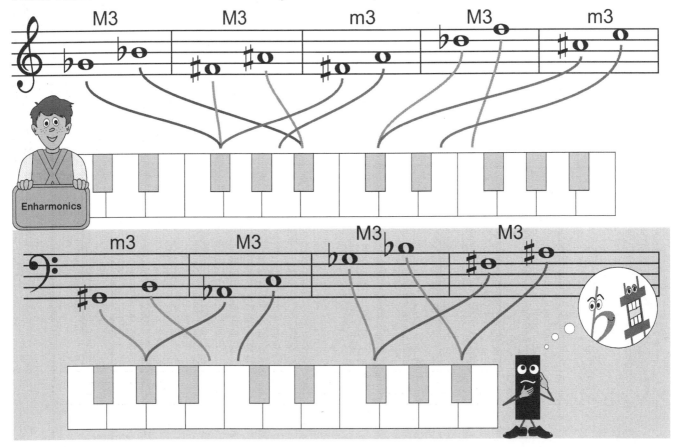

Doctor Mozart Music Theory Workbook, Answers for Level 2 & 3.  © MMVIII, MMXV Machiko and Paul Christopher Musgrave.    Published by April Avenue Music.    www.DoctorMozart.com

# Major 3rds Up and Down Quiz

On the staff and keyboard, write a major 3rd *down* from each paw print. Draw lines.

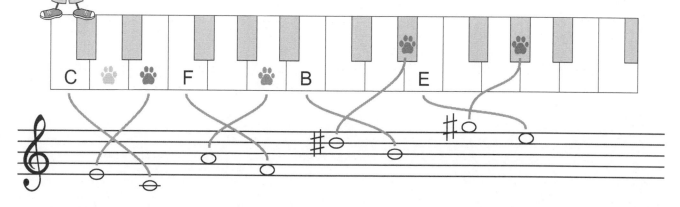

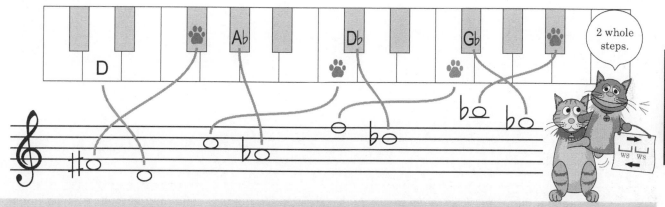

Next, write a major 3rd *up* from each paw print. Write the 3rds on the staff. Draw lines.

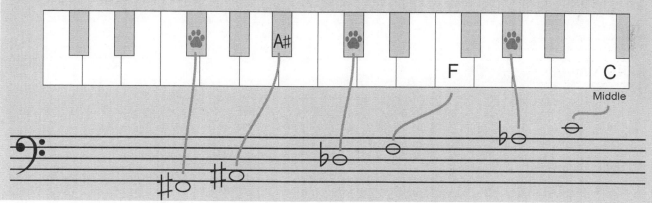

Write a major 3rd above or below each given note, according to the direction of the arrows.

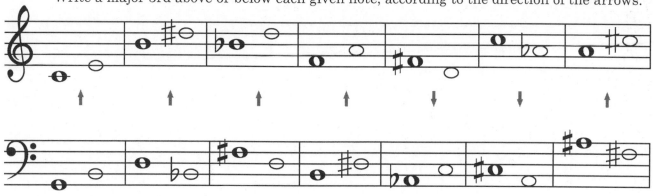

# Minor 3rds Up & Down Quiz

On the staff and keyboard, write a minor 3rd *down* from each paw print. Draw lines.

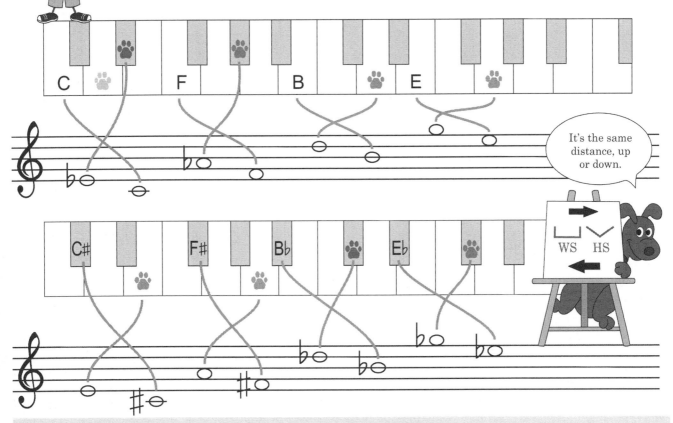

It's the same distance, up or down.

WS    HS

Next, write minor 3rds *up* from each paw print. Write the 3rds on the staff too. Draw lines.

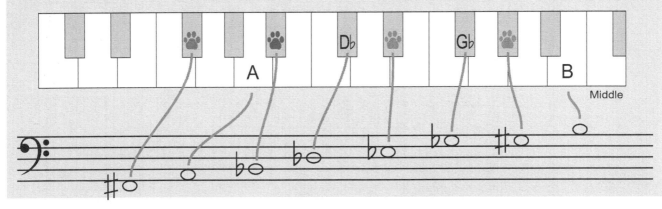

Write a minor 3rd above or below each given note, according to the direction of the arrows.

# How Can a 4th be Perfect?

Trace the gray brackets and text. How many cats are there between the red paw prints? __2__

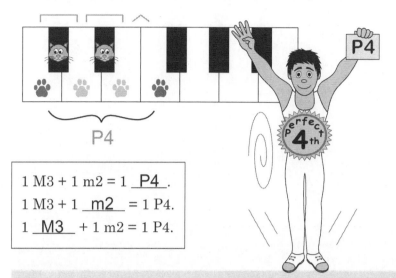

P4

1 M3 + 1 m2 = 1 __P4__ .
1 M3 + 1 __m2__ = 1 P4.
1 __M3__ + 1 m2 = 1 P4.

The red paw prints span a perfect 4th, or P4. This perfect 4th spans

__2__ whole steps plus __1__ half step. In other words, this perfect 4th spans

a major 3rd plus a __minor__ 2nd. A perfect 4th is one half step

larger than a major __3rd__.

We never say that a 4th is major or minor. Instead, we say 4ths are *perfect*. The symbol for perfect 4th is P4.

P4 means __perfect__ __4th__.

Every perfect 4th spans 4 notes, known as a tetrachord. A tetrachord contains __4__ notes. Below, each set of colored boxes shows a P4 tetrachord. Name the keys. Use adjacent alphabet letters. Draw square and V brackets.

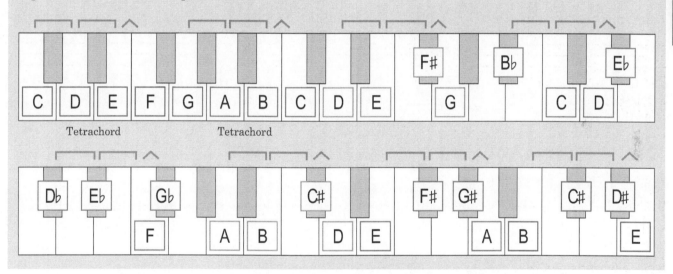

Next, name the keys to show the tetrachords. Draw square and V brackets. Write P4 under each perfect 4th. Write each P4 on the staff. Draw lines.

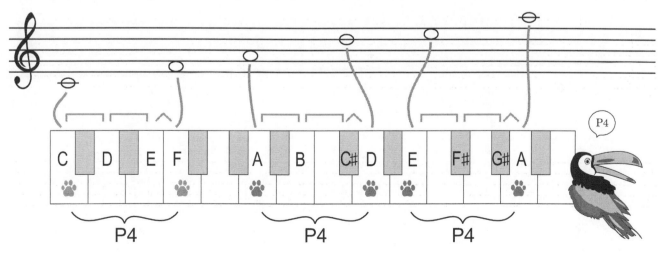

Doctor Mozart Music Theory Workbook, Answers for Level 2 & 3. © MMVIII, MMXV Machiko and Paul Christopher Musgrave. Published by April Avenue Music. www.DoctorMozart.com

# Perfect 5ths

Trace these brackets.

C  D  E  F      F  G  C  D  E  F  G

⊔  ⊔  ⌄  +  ⊔  =  ⊔  ⊔  ⌄  ⊔

A perfect 4th   +   1 whole step   =   a perfect 5th.

A perfect 5th is one __whole__ step larger than a perfect 4th.

**P5** is the symbol for perfect 5th.

Trace the brackets on the keyboard.

---

Each set of colored boxes shows a P5. Name the keys. Use adjacent alphabet letters. Draw square and V brackets.

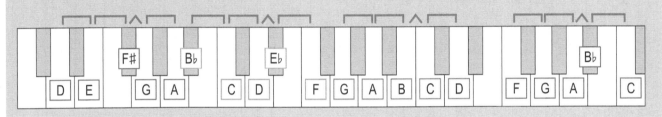

D  E  | F#  G  A  | Bb  C  D  | Eb  F  G  A  B  C  D  | F  G  A  | Bb  C

---

At right, circle each group of brackets that represents a P5.

A perfect 5th spans 5 alphabet letters.

In a P5, the whole and half steps can be in any order, but they must add up to 3½ steps. Circle each group of brackets that makes a P5.

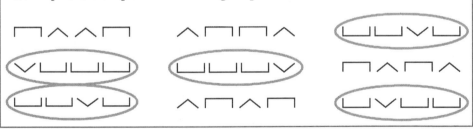

---

Next, each colored box is the bottom note of a P5. Name the white keys spanned by each P5. Draw brackets. They will not be in the usual order.

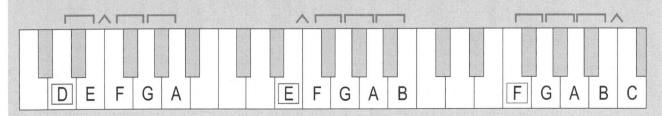

D  E  F  G  A        E  F  G  A  B        F  G  A  B  C

Doctor Mozart Music Theory Workbook, Answers for Level 2 & 3.  © MMVIII, MMXV Machiko and Paul Christopher Musgrave.    Published by April Avenue Music.    www.DoctorMozart.com

# Harmonic & Melodic Intervals

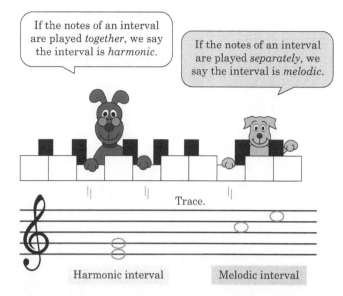

If the notes of an interval are played *together*, we say the interval is *harmonic*.

If the notes of an interval are played *separately*, we say the interval is *melodic*.

Trace.

Harmonic interval

Melodic interval

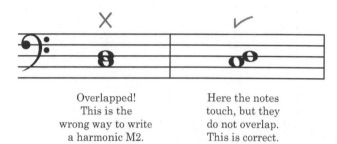

When writing a harmonic 2nd, do not allow the notes to overlap. Instead, write the notes very close together. Look at these examples:

✗

✔

Overlapped! This is the wrong way to write a harmonic M2.

Here the notes touch, but they do not overlap. This is correct.

**2 B**

Name these harmonic intervals. Draw lines to the keyboard.

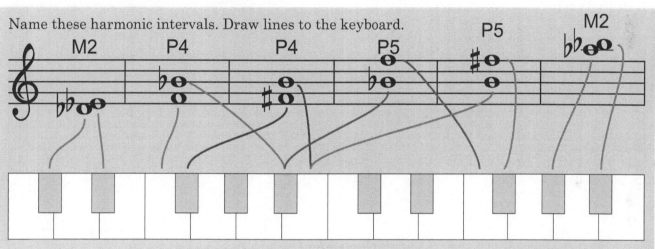

Above each given note, write the harmonic interval indicated. Draw lines to the keyboard.

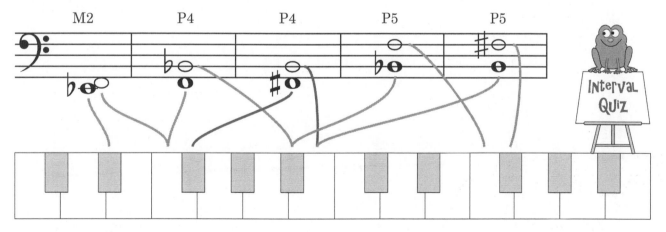

Interval Quiz

Write the correct clef in each bar to make each interval a perfect 4th.

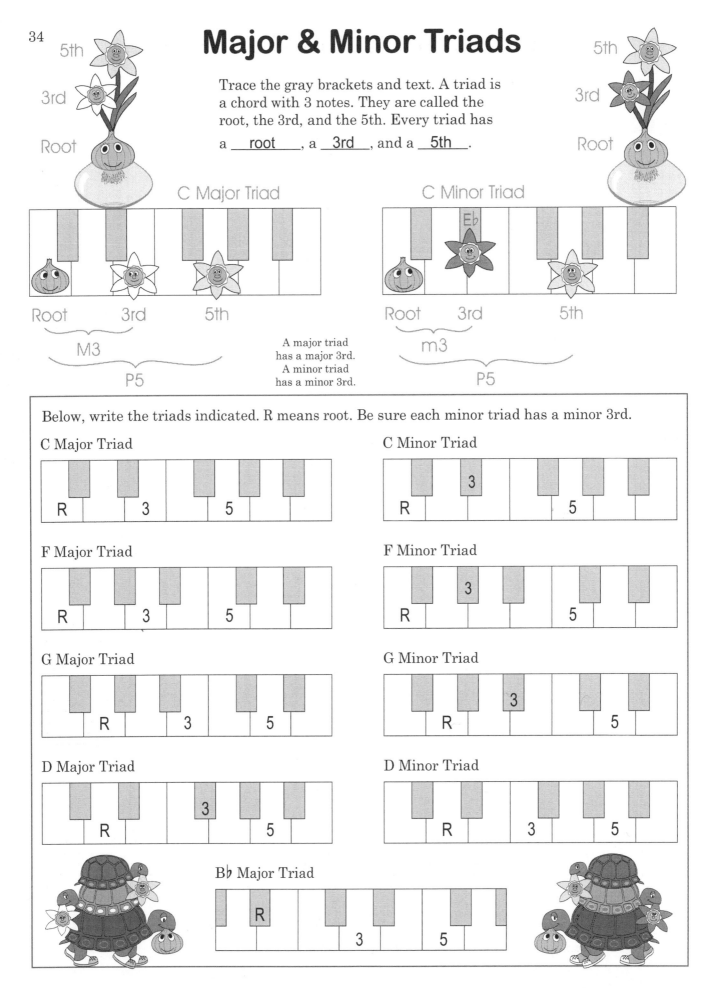

# Major & Minor Triads

Trace the gray brackets and text. A triad is
a chord with 3 notes. They are called the
root, the 3rd, and the 5th. Every triad has
a __root__ , a __3rd__ , and a __5th__ .

# Tonic, Subdominant & Dominant

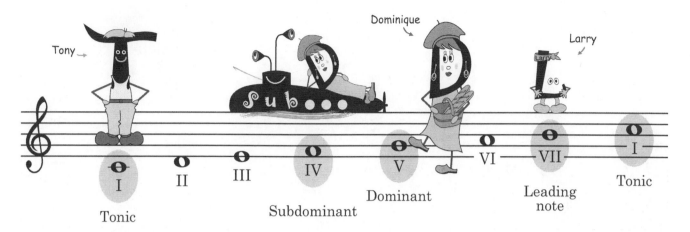

The 1st degree of the scale is called the _____ **Tonic** _____
The 5th degree of the scale is called the _____ **Dominant** _____
The 4th degree of the scale is called the _____ **Subdominant** _____

*The 7 notes of the scale are called degrees of the scale.*

**2 B**

Below, draw lines from each Roman numeral to the matching name.

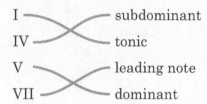

I — subdominant
IV — tonic
V — leading note
VII — dominant

Name these degrees of the scale.

I ........... **Tonic**
IV .......... **Subdominant**
V ........... **Dominant**
VII ......... **leading note**

Next, write an ascending G major scale, using accidentals. Number the notes with Roman numerals. Name the tonic, subdominant, dominant, and leading notes. Draw square and V brackets.

*This car's tail lights look like the whole and half steps in a scale.*

Tetrachord   Whole step   Tetrachord

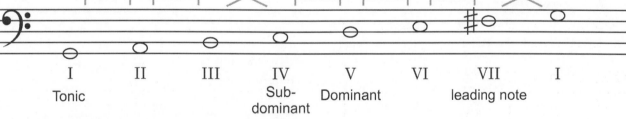

I    II    III    IV    V    VI    VII    I
Tonic              Sub-  Dominant      leading note
                   dominant

Now do the same with a F major scale.

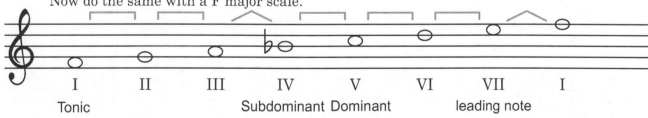

I    II    III    IV    V    VI    VII    I
Tonic              Subdominant Dominant      leading note

The 7 notes of the scale are called _____ **degrees** _____ of the scale.

Roman numerals are often written with a stroke across the top and bottom.

Doctor Mozart Music Theory Workbook, Answers for Level 2 & 3.   © MMVIII, MMXV Machiko and Paul Christopher Musgrave.   Published by April Avenue Music.   www.DoctorMozart.com

# Dominant & Subdominant Triads

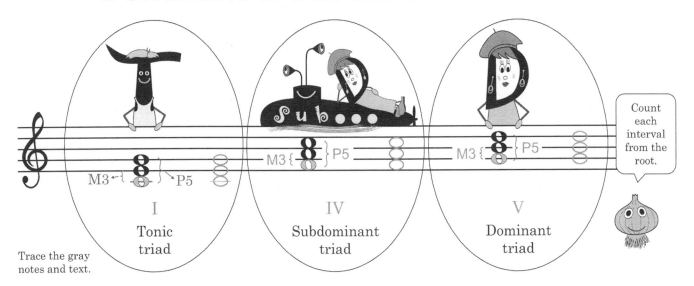

I
Tonic
triad

IV
Subdominant
triad

V
Dominant
triad

Count each interval from the root.

Trace the gray notes and text.

The chords shown above are the primary triads of the C major scale. They are on I, IV, and V.

The primary triads are on I, IV, and __V__ in every scale.

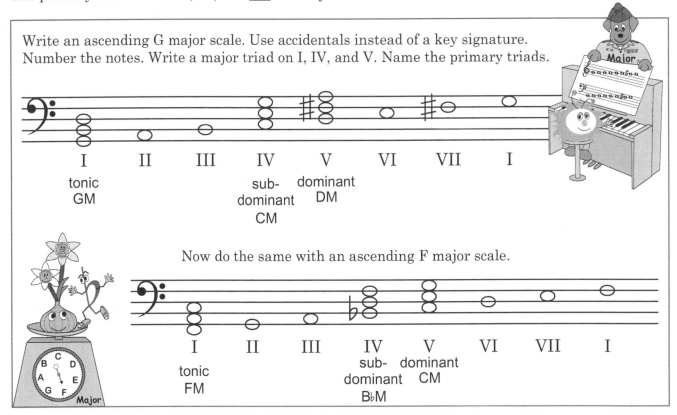

Write an ascending G major scale. Use accidentals instead of a key signature. Number the notes. Write a major triad on I, IV, and V. Name the primary triads.

I    II    III    IV    V    VI    VII    I

tonic
GM

sub-
dominant
CM

dominant
DM

Now do the same with an ascending F major scale.

I    II    III    IV    V    VI    VII    I

tonic
FM

sub-
dominant
B♭M

dominant
CM

Write the correct Roman numeral under each triad.

In the C major scale.

In the F major scale.

In the G major scale.

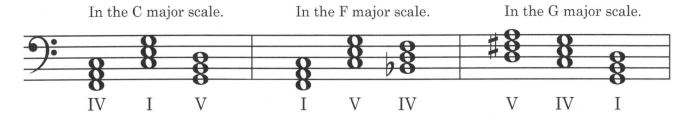

IV    I    V        I    V    IV        V    IV    I

Doctor Mozart Music Theory Workbook, Answers for Level 2 & 3.  © MMVIII, MMXV Machiko and Paul Christopher Musgrave.    Published by April Avenue Music.    www.DoctorMozart.com

Write a single rest at each X to complete the bars. Number the beats.

Write the correct clef for each group of primary triads.

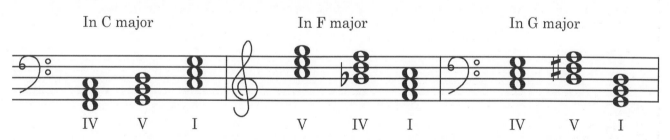

Write Roman numerals in the blanks to match each triad with the scales listed below it.
If there is no correct answer, write an X.

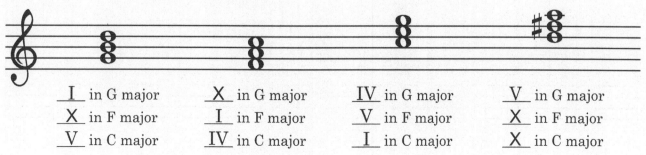

Doctor Mozart Music Theory Workbook, Answers for Level 2 & 3.  © MMVIII, MMXV Machiko and Paul Christopher Musgrave.  Published by April Avenue Music.  www.DoctorMozart.com

# Expert Review

Write the correct clef on each staff to make every interval either an m3 or P5.

Which clef?

Which clef?

Next, name the intervals. Is every minor 3rd followed by a major 3rd? __no__

M3   m3   M3   m3   M3   m3   m3   M3   m3   M3   m3

Make two grand staffs, each with a different time signature. Fill some bars with any notes and rests you like. Include some 2nds, 3rds, 4ths, and 5ths. Also include some eighth rests. Write some of the musical terms and signs you have learned too. Number the beats.

Doctor Mozart Music Theory Workbook, Answers for Level 2 & 3.   © MMVIII, MMXV Machiko and Paul Christopher Musgrave.   Published by April Avenue Music.   www.DoctorMozart.com

# Doctor Mozart® Music Theory Workbook

## In-Depth Piano Theory Fun for Music Lessons and Home Schooling

### Level 2C - Contents

Every day, start by reviewing what you learned the day before. Then complete a page or two, and you will make good progress.

Highly Effective for Children Learning a Musical Instrument.

2 C

Doctor Mozart workbooks are filled with friendly cartoon characters. They make it fun to learn music theory in-depth. And in-depth music theory knowledge is essential for children learning a musical instrument. Use Doctor Mozart workbooks by themselves or with other teaching materials. Use them for music lessons and for home schooling.

The authors, Machiko and Paul Musgrave, are both graduates of Juilliard. Machiko has taught piano and theory at Soai University in Japan. Paul is an Associate of the Royal Conservatory of Music. The authors hope you enjoy using this book!

**Copyright laws protect the right of authors and publishers to earn a living from their work. Please respect these laws, and pay for the books you use and enjoy. Photocopying or reproducing this book in any manner may lead to prosecution.**

Many thanks to Kevin Musgrave for his meticulous proof-reading and insightful suggestions.
Created by Machiko and Paul Christopher Musgrave. Illustrated by Machiko Yamane Musgrave.

Version 1.0.5
Doctor Mozart Music Theory Workbook, Answers for Level 2 & 3.   © MMVIII, MMXV Machiko and Paul Christopher Musgrave.   Published by April Avenue Music.   www.DoctorMozart.com

# Octaves and Unisons

The two pink keys are 8 notes apart. They form an octave, or P8.

Are the two green keys one octave apart? __Yes__

The symbol for octave is __P__ 8.

An octave is an interval that spans __8__ alphabet letters on the keyboard. Circle each pair of letters that could form an octave:

(C C)   G A   (B♭ B♭)   H H   (F♯ F♯)

Octaves are perfect, not major.

Octave = P8

---

Name the following notes. Then write notes in between to make octaves.

F   G   A   B♭

F   G   A   B♭

---

Name these intervals.

P8   M2   P8   M3   P8   M2   P8   P5   P8

---

Unison = P1

What is a unison? If two instruments play the same note at the same time, then we say they are playing a unison. Below, write several unisons and octaves. Use some accidentals. When writing unisons, write the two notes *beside* each other.

Unison P1

The symbol for perfect unison is P1.

# Italian Musical Terms

**con pedale** means play *with pedal.*

*con ped.* is the abbreviation.

Push the pedal down. 𝓟𝓮𝓭. (Ped.) ✳ Release the pedal.

When you see one of these pedal marks, use the pedal on the right (the sustain pedal).

ottava (8va)

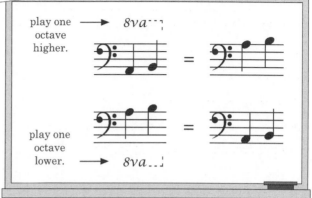

8va means play the notes one octave higher or lower. Here's how:

play one octave higher. → 8va

play one octave lower. → 8va

8va is short for *ottava*, which is Italian for *octave.*

A *tenuto* sign ( − ) tells you to hold the note for its full normal duration, or slightly longer.

The abbreviation for tenuto is *ten.*

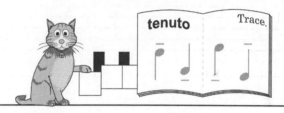

mano sinistra — M.S. left hand

M.D. right hand — mano destra

tenuto | Trace.

---

**Write a word or sign in each blank.**

The Italian word for octave: <u>ottava</u>

Hold the note for its full length: <u>tenuto</u>

Use the sustain pedal: <u>con pedale</u>

Play with your right hand: <u>M.D.</u>

Play with your left hand: <u>M.S.</u>

**2 C**

Do these pedal marks 𝓟𝓮𝓭. ✳ have the same meaning as this pedal mark? ⌐_⌐ <u>Yes</u>

Next, look at the signs. Then write the actual notes on the lower staff.

# White key
# Enharmonics

In the colored boxes, name each key two different ways. Write the notes on the staff. Draw lines.

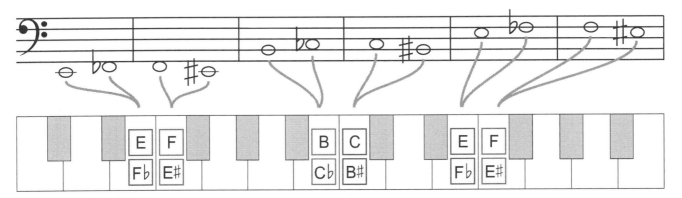

Draw lines from the printed notes to the keys. In the empty bars, write the enharmonic equivalents. Then draw lines from the new notes to the keyboard.

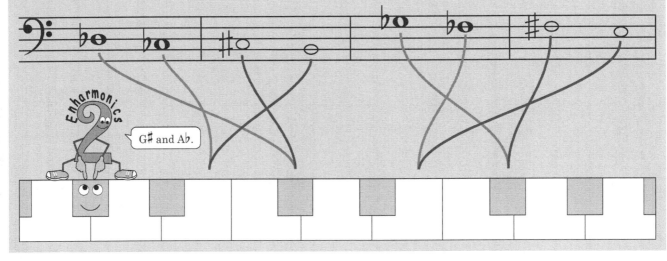

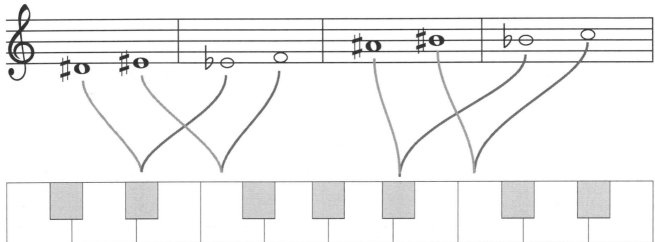

Doctor Mozart Music Theory Workbook, Answers for Level 2 & 3. © MMVIII, MMXV Machiko and Paul Christopher Musgrave.    Published by April Avenue Music.    www.DoctorMozart.com

# Interval Review

Write neighboring alphabet letters in the boxes. For each interval, label the white keys first, then the black keys. Draw a square bracket at each whole step. Draw a V bracket at each half step. Name the intervals.

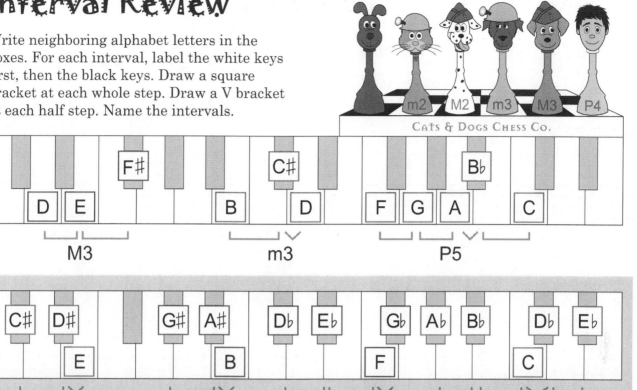

How many letter names does each of these intervals span? m2 **2** M2 **2** m3 **3** M3 **3** P4 **4**

Name the keys to show the intervals. Start at each labeled key, and go up. Draw brackets.

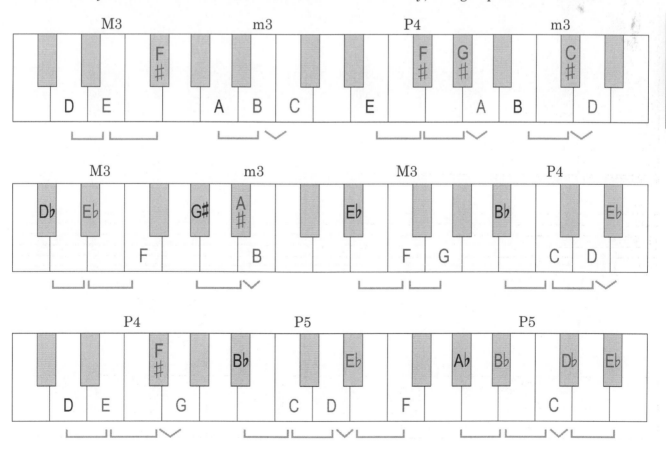

# Black Key Intervals

Name the intervals.
Draw lines to the keyboard.

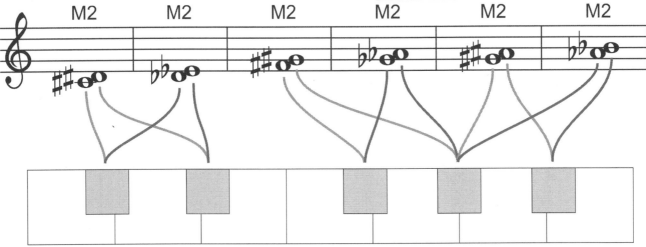

On this staff, write a harmonic M2 above each given note. Draw lines.

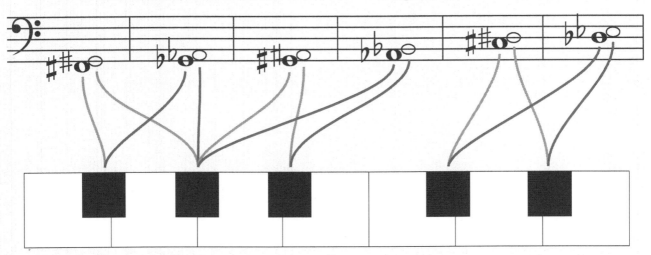

Write a harmonic interval above each note, as indicated. Draw lines.

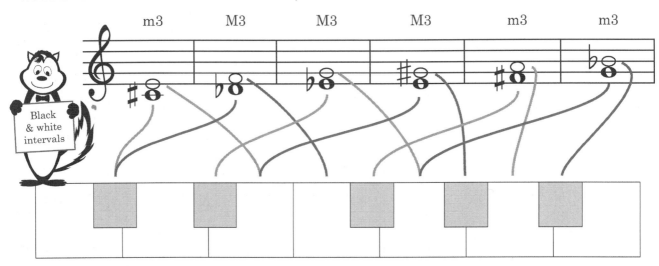

Doctor Mozart Music Theory Workbook, Answers for Level 2 & 3.  © MMVIII, MMXV  Machiko and Paul Christopher Musgrave.    Published by April Avenue Music.    www.DoctorMozart.com

# The D Major Scale and Primary Triads

The Roman numerals on this keyboard show a D Major scale.
Draw square and V brackets. Which keys are black? __F#__ and __C#__

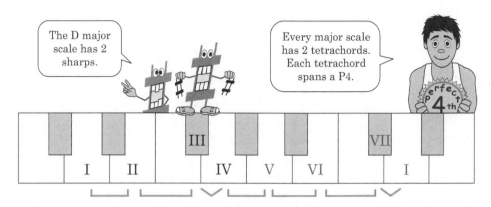

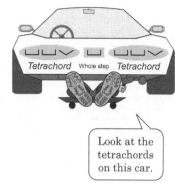

Write a triad on I, IV, and V. Draw square and V brackets. Draw lines.

**Review**

The triads on I, IV, and V are called primary triads.

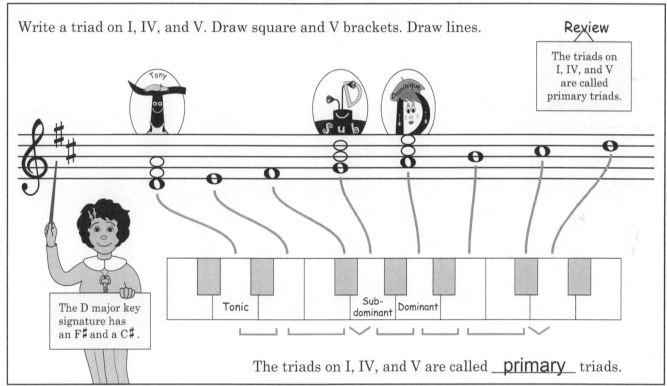

The triads on I, IV, and V are called __primary__ triads.

On the staff below, write a D major key signature. Write an ascending D major scale. Write the primary triads. Draw lines from the scale notes to the keys.

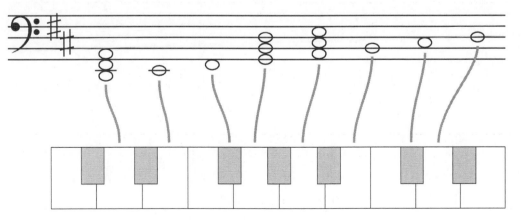

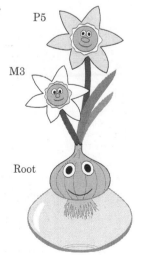

P5

M3

Root

Doctor Mozart Music Theory Workbook, Answers for Level 2 & 3.  © MMVIII, MMXV Machiko and Paul Christopher Musgrave.   Published by April Avenue Music.   www.DoctorMozart.com

# The B Flat Major Scale and Primary Triads

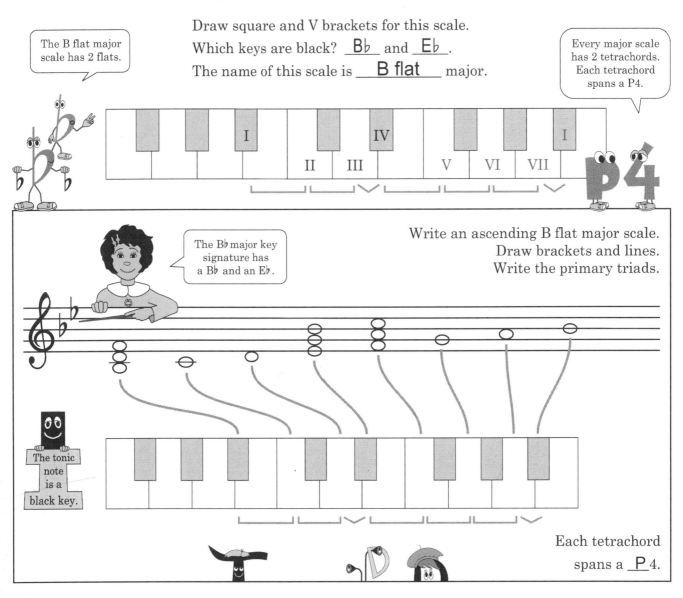

Draw square and V brackets for this scale.
Which keys are black? __B♭__ and __E♭__.
The name of this scale is ___B flat___ major.

The B flat major scale has 2 flats.

Every major scale has 2 tetrachords. Each tetrachord spans a P4.

Write an ascending B flat major scale.
Draw brackets and lines.
Write the primary triads.

The B♭ major key signature has a B♭ and an E♭.

The tonic note is a black key.

Each tetrachord spans a __P__4.

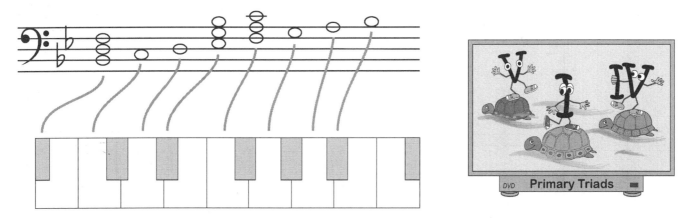

Write a B flat major key signature and scale on the staff. Write the primary triads. Draw lines.

The word adjacent means neighboring. For example, in the alphabet, the letter A is adjacent to B.
But A is not adjacent to C. An alternate word for neighboring is _____adjacent_____.
Adjacent is pronounced a-JAY-cent. Adjacent means _____neighboring_____.

Doctor Mozart Music Theory Workbook, Answers for Level 2 & 3.  © MMVIII, MMXV  Machiko and Paul Christopher Musgrave.    Published by April Avenue Music.    www.DoctorMozart.com

# Compare These Scales

Name the major scale that you could play on each keyboard, using only the colored keys. Write I, IV, and V on the correct keys. Name each colored black key. Draw lines between the keyboards to show which notes differ across the adjacent scales.

Which keys are different?

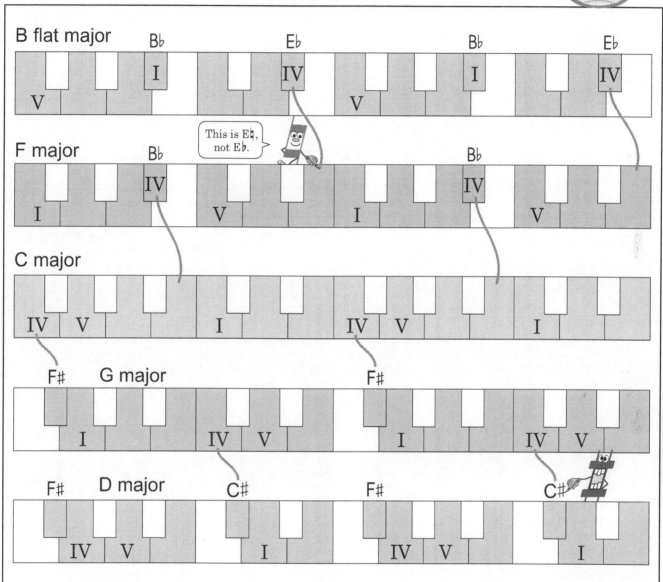

Circle all the scales that each note belongs to. For example, E *natural* can be found in all of the scales listed below it, except B flat major. In contrast, E *flat* belongs to just one of the scales listed.

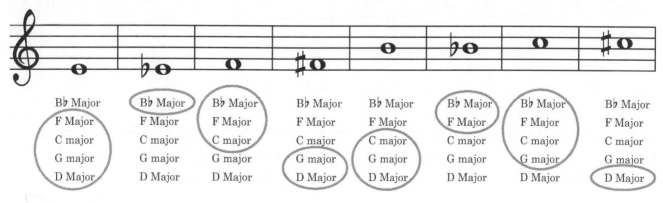

Doctor Mozart Music Theory Workbook, Answers for Level 2 & 3.  © MMVIII, MMXV Machiko and Paul Christopher Musgrave.  Published by April Avenue Music.  www.DoctorMozart.com

# How to Remember Key Signatures

Trace and name these key signatures. Then write each key signature on your own.

__Bb__ major    __D__ major    __Bb__ major    __D__ major

The flats in B flat major are __B__ and __E__. Remember them with the phrase *Battle Ends*.

The sharps in D major are __F__ and __C__. Remember them with the phrase *Father Charles*.

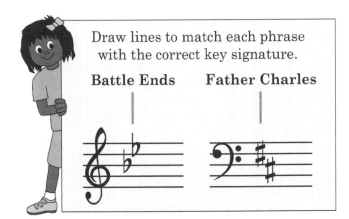

Draw lines to match each phrase with the correct key signature.

**Battle Ends**    **Father Charles**

The sharps and flats in each key signature are always written in the same order.

FATHER CHARLES

You can remember the B flat major key signature with two words: __Battle__ __Ends__

You can remember the D major key signature with two words: __Father__ __Charles__

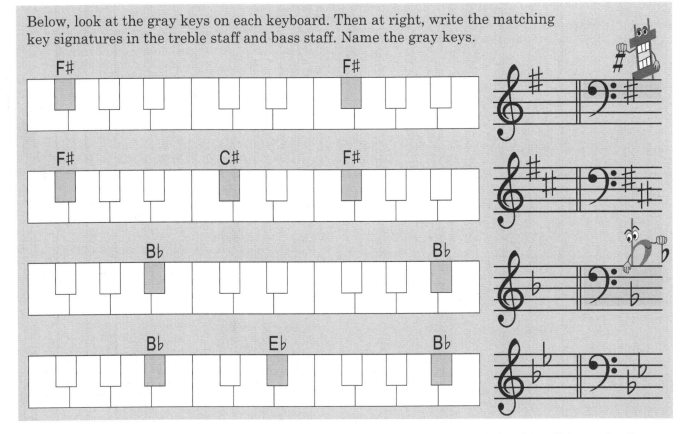

Below, look at the gray keys on each keyboard. Then at right, write the matching key signatures in the treble staff and bass staff. Name the gray keys.

# What is a Key?

The word *key* has two musical meanings: →

Name these intervals. Then on the right side of each staff, write the key signature that matches the accidentals. Name the key. Write the primary triads.

M3   M2   M3   m2   m3   The key: **G major**

m3   M3   m3   M2   M3   The key: **D major**

P4   m2   P4   M2   M2   The key: **F major**

m2   m3   P5   M3   m2   The key: **B♭ major**

Write the correct clef for each key signature. Name each key signature. Circle each note that should be played with a black key. Name the intervals.

**Key Signatures at Work**

**B flat major**

m2   P4   m2

**B flat major**

M3   P5   M2

**D major**

M2   M2   m2

**D major**

m2   M3   M2

2C

# Triad Test

Write R, 3, and 5 to show the root, 3rd, and 5th of each triad.

**I in B flat major**

R    3    5

**I in D major**

3    R    5

**IV in B flat major**

R    3    5

**IV in D major**

R    3    5

**V in B flat major**

R    3    5

**V in D major**

R    3    5

---

Write the correct clef for each key signature. Then name the key signatures.

F Major    D Major    G Major    D Major    B♭ Major    B♭ Major

---

Dominant    Subdominant    Tonic

Write the correct clef for each key signature.
Then write a triad for each Roman numeral.

V    IV    I

V    IV    I

V    IV    I

V    IV    I

Write a harmonic interval above each note as indicated. Draw lines to the keyboard.

# Black & White 3rds

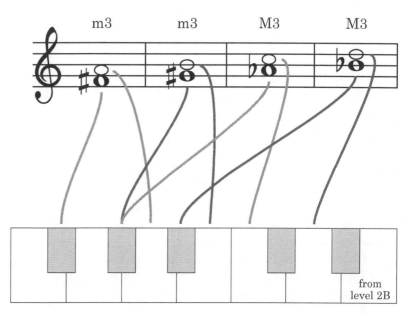

m3    m3    M3    M3

from level 2B

Write a harmonic interval **below** each note as indicated. Draw lines.

m3         m3         M3         M3

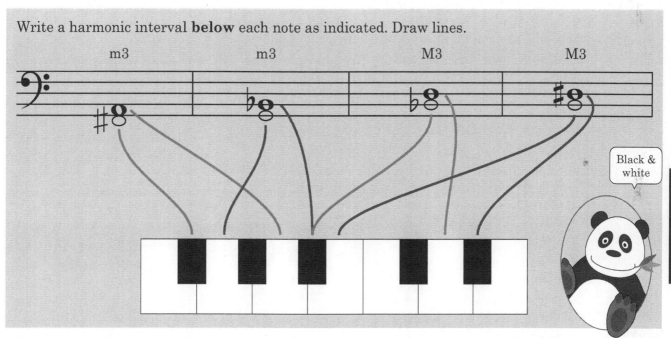

Black & white

2 C

Below, write any accidentals needed to make each interval a P5. Then write a major 3rd above each bottom note to form a major triad. Use the keyboard to help find the intervals.

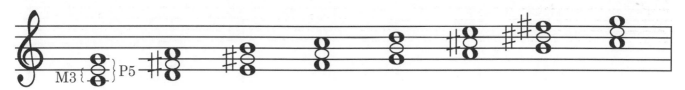

M3{ }P5

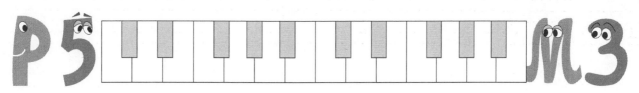

Doctor Mozart Music Theory Workbook, Answers for Level 2 & 3. © MMVIII, MMXV  Machiko and Paul Christopher Musgrave.    Published by April Avenue Music.    www.DoctorMozart.com

# Black & White 4ths & 5ths

Zebra intervals have one black key and one white key.

Every P4 contains 2½ steps. You can count them in any order. On this staff, write a P4 above each given note. Draw lines. Circle the zebra intervals.

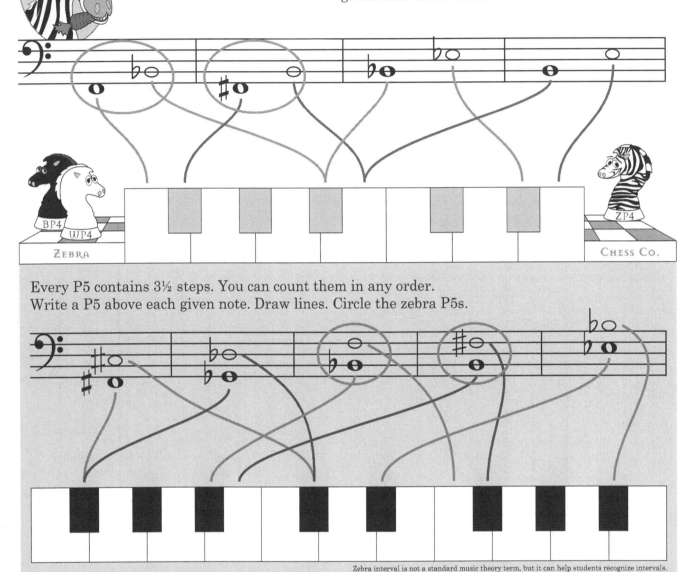

Every P5 contains 3½ steps. You can count them in any order. Write a P5 above each given note. Draw lines. Circle the zebra P5s.

Zebra interval is not a standard music theory term, but it can help students recognize intervals.

Write two different zebra P5s and two different zebra P4s. Draw lines.

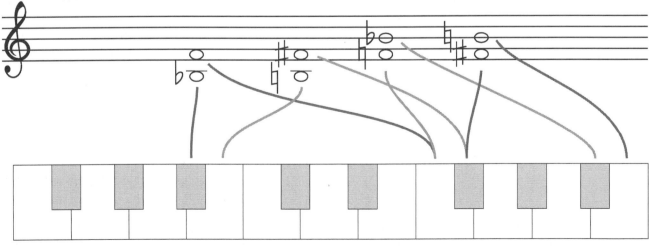

# Natural Minor Scales

Write Roman numerals to complete these two scales. Use only white keys. Draw a V bracket at each semitone. Which scale has a semitone between II and III? __The A natural minor scale__.

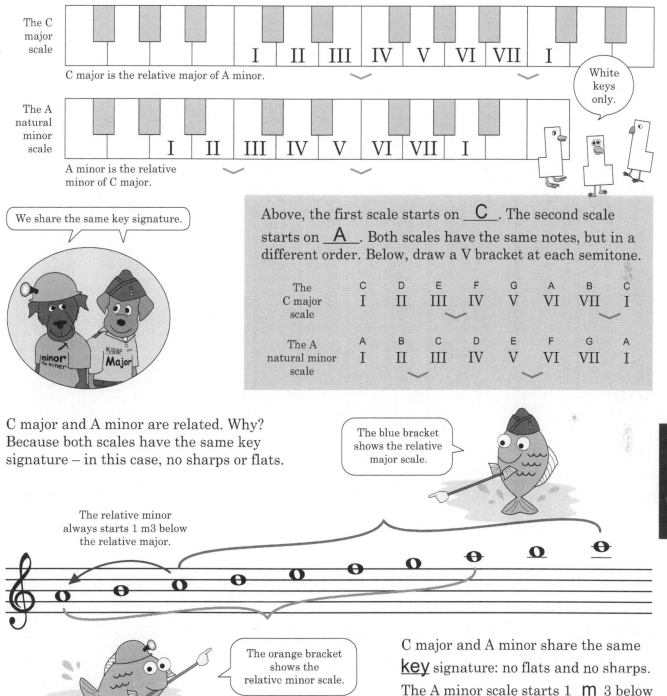

The C major scale

I  II  III  IV  V  VI  VII  I

C major is the relative major of A minor.

White keys only.

The A natural minor scale

I  II  III  IV  V  VI  VII  I

A minor is the relative minor of C major.

We share the same key signature.

minor
the miner

Major

Above, the first scale starts on __C__. The second scale starts on __A__. Both scales have the same notes, but in a different order. Below, draw a V bracket at each semitone.

| The C major scale | C | D | E | F | G | A | B | C |
|---|---|---|---|---|---|---|---|---|
| | I | II | III | IV | V | VI | VII | I |

| The A natural minor scale | A | B | C | D | E | F | G | A |
|---|---|---|---|---|---|---|---|---|
| | I | II | III | IV | V | VI | VII | I |

C major and A minor are related. Why? Because both scales have the same key signature – in this case, no sharps or flats.

The blue bracket shows the relative major scale.

The relative minor always starts 1 m3 below the relative major.

The orange bracket shows the relative minor scale.

C major and A minor share the same __key__ signature: no flats and no sharps.

The A minor scale starts 1 __m__ 3 below the C major scale tonic.

Next, each named key is the tonic of a major scale. Label the relative minor tonic with a lower case letter. Draw an arrow to connect each pair of tonic notes.

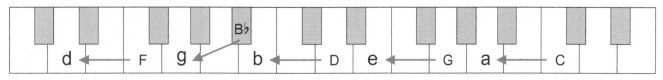

d ← F    g    B♭    b ← D    e ← G    a ← C

Doctor Mozart Music Theory Workbook, Answers for Level 2 & 3.  © MMVIII, MMXV  Machiko and Paul Christopher Musgrave.    Published by April Avenue Music.    www.DoctorMozart.com

2C

# Relative Major & Minor Scale Quiz

Name the notes in each scale.
Mark each semitone with a V bracket.

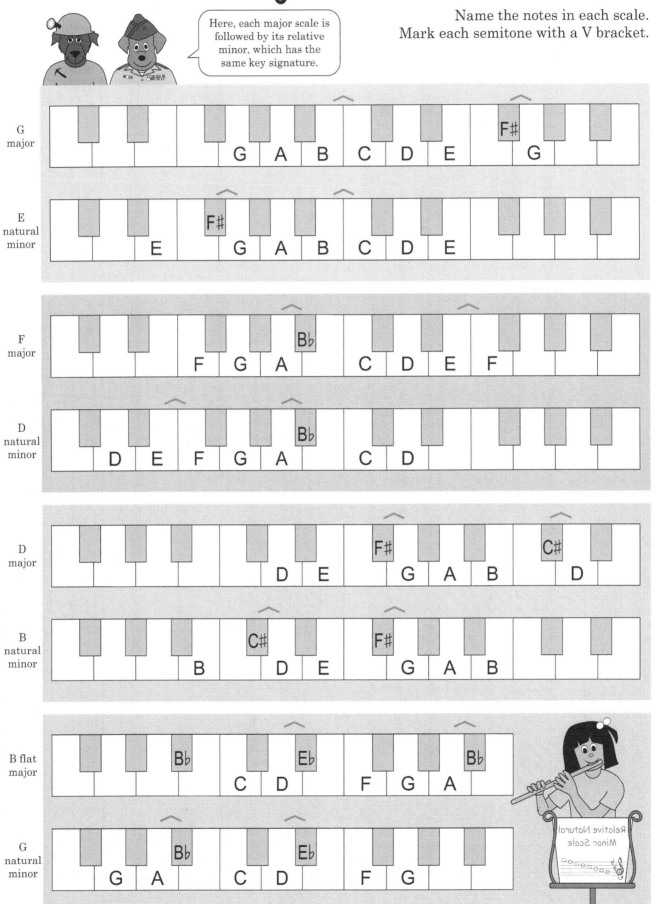

# More Relatives

Write the correct key signatures.
Write the scales, ascending. Draw lines.

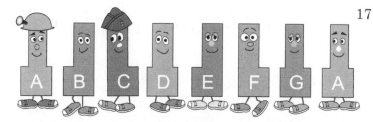

D major

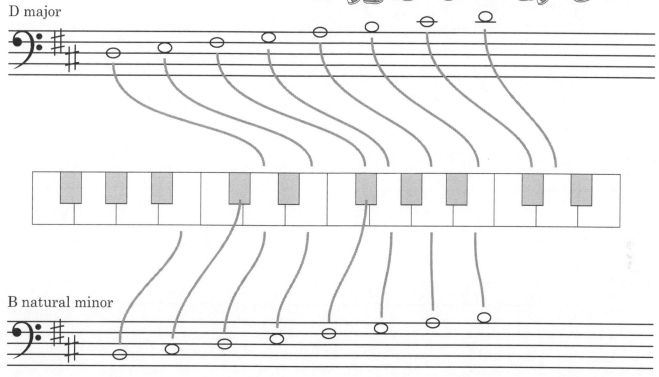

B natural minor

B♭ major

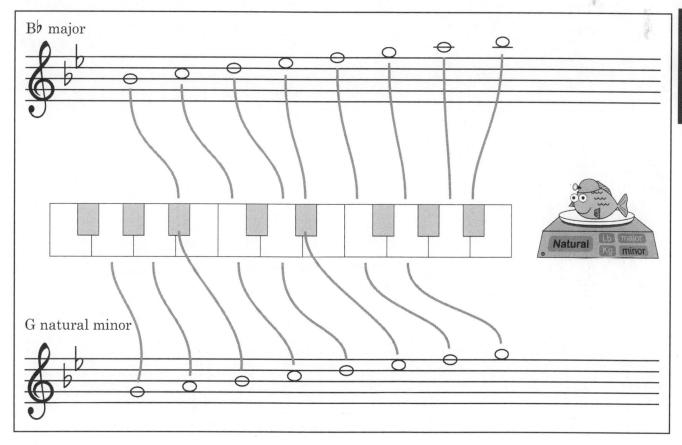

G natural minor

2C

Doctor Mozart Music Theory Workbook, Answers for Level 2 & 3.   © MMVIII, MMXV  Machiko and Paul Christopher Musgrave.   Published by April Avenue Music.   www.DoctorMozart.com

# Key Signature Quiz

Draw lines to match each phrase with the correct key signature.

Father Charles      B♭ major

Battle Ends      D major

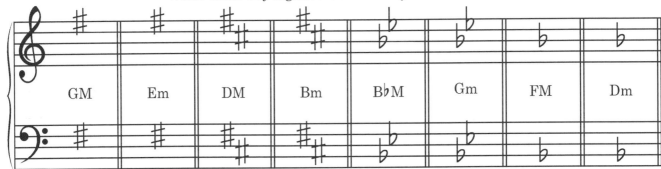

Write these key signatures. M = major. m = minor.

| GM | Em | DM | Bm | B♭M | Gm | FM | Dm |
|----|----|----|----|-----|----|----|----|

Each printed note is the tonic note of a minor scale. Write the correct key signatures. Name them. Use no more than 2 sharps or 2 flats.

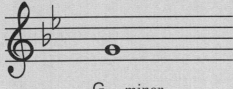

__G__ minor

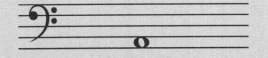

__B__ minor

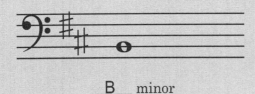

__B__ minor

__A__ minor

Write the correct clefs. Name each key signature two ways: As a major key, and as the relative minor.

__G__ major __E__ minor     __B♭__ major __G__ minor     __D__ major __B__ minor     __F__ major __D__ minor

Doctor Mozart Music Theory Workbook, Answers for Level 2 & 3.   © MMVIII, MMXV  Machiko and Paul Christopher Musgrave.    Published by April Avenue Music.    www.DoctorMozart.com

# How to Invert Intervals

Each of these keyboards has an orange paw interval.
If you raise the lowest paw note by one octave, you
can make the blue paw interval. Name the intervals.

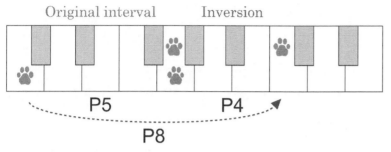

Original interval       Inversion

P5          P4

P8

To invert an interval,
raise the lowest note
by an octave.

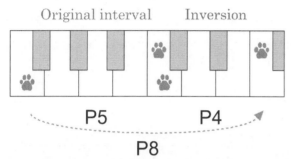

Original interval    Inversion

P5          P4

P8

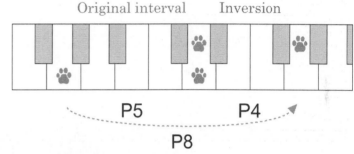

Original interval    Inversion

P5          P4

P8

To invert an interval, raise the lowest note by an _____octave_____ .

Next, for each paw print interval, let's raise the lowest note by an octave.
Label the keys that form each inversion. Name the intervals.

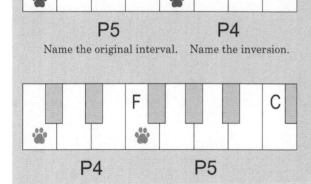

G          C

P5          P4

Name the original interval.    Name the inversion.

F          C

P4          P5

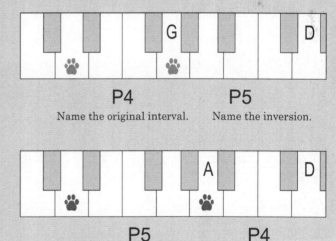

G          D

P4          P5

Name the original interval.    Name the inversion.

A          D

P5          P4

2
C

Invert up!

Invert each interval. Name the intervals.

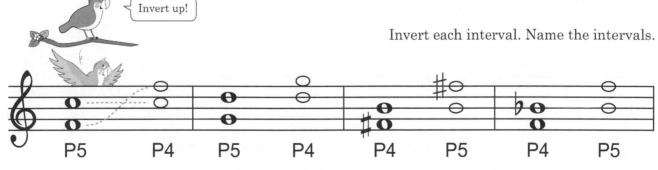

P5    P4    P5    P4    P4    P5    P4    P5

Doctor Mozart Music Theory Workbook, Answers for Level 2 & 3.   © MMVIII, MMXV  Machiko and Paul Christopher Musgrave.    Published by April Avenue Music.   www.DoctorMozart.com

# How to Invert Downward

To invert an interval downward, lower the highest note by a P8.

Lower the highest note by an octave.

Invert each of these paw print intervals downward. Label the keys that form each inversion. Name the intervals.

**P8**

C    F    E    B
P4    P5    P5    P4
P8    P8

F    C    B♭    E♭
P5    P4    P4    P5
P8    P8

F♯    B    B    F♯
P4    P5    P5    P4
P8    P8

Invert each interval downward. Name the intervals.

P4    P5    P4    P5    P5    P4    P5    P4

Below, draw lines to connect the green Zs. Name the intervals.
Draw lines to connect the red Zs. Name the intervals.

Zebra 4ths and 5ths.

P4    P5    P4    P5
Z    Z    Z    Z    Z
Z    Z    Z    Z    Z
P4    P5    P4    P5

Doctor Mozart Music Theory Workbook, Answers for Level 2 & 3. © MMVIII, MMXV Machiko and Paul Christopher Musgrave.    Published by April Avenue Music.    www.DoctorMozart.com

# Which is Bigger: P5 or M6?

Write the note names in the boxes. Use neighboring letters. Draw brackets.

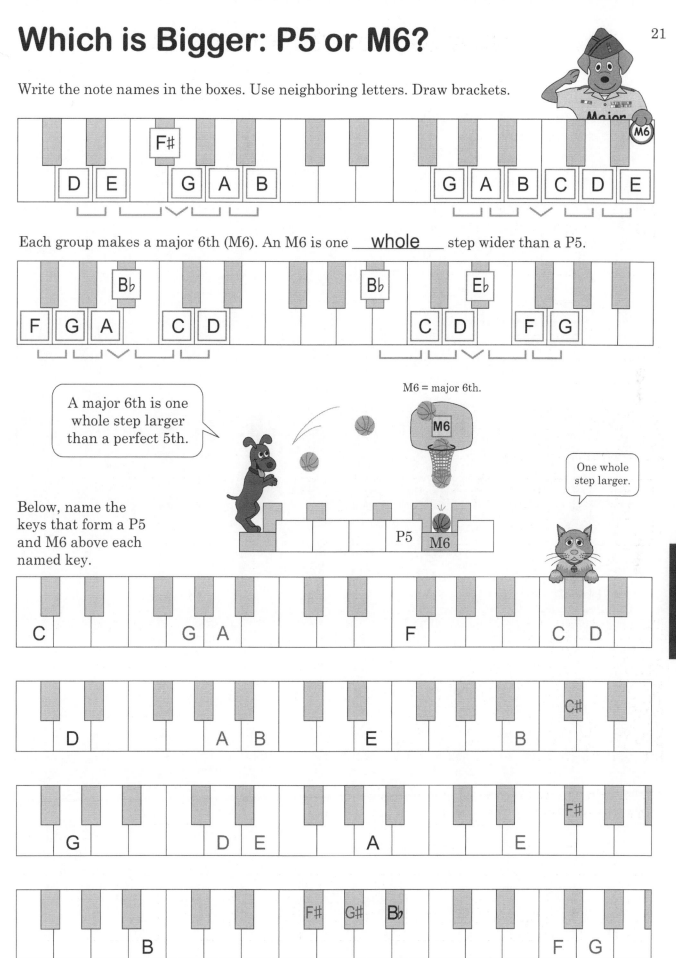

Each group makes a major 6th (M6). An M6 is one ___whole___ step wider than a P5.

> A major 6th is one whole step larger than a perfect 5th.

M6 = major 6th.

> One whole step larger.

Below, name the keys that form a P5 and M6 above each named key.

2 C

# A Smaller 6th

A minor 6th is one half step smaller than a major 6th. At right, trace the arrow and brackets. Below, draw an arrow from each right paw to show a minor 6th.

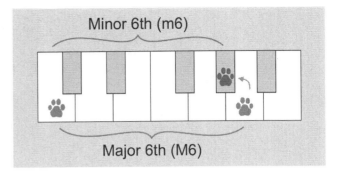

Minor 6th (m6)

Major 6th (M6)

One half step smaller.

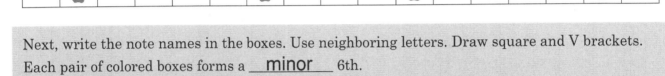

Next, write the note names in the boxes. Use neighboring letters. Draw square and V brackets.
Each pair of colored boxes forms a ___minor___ 6th.

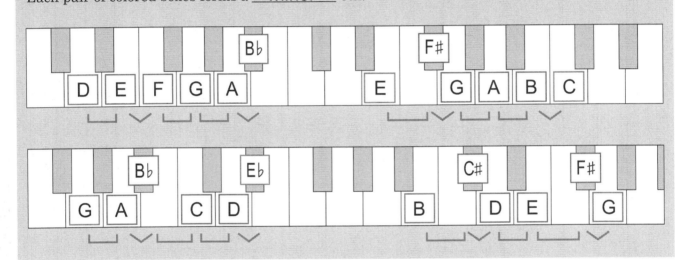

Mark a P5, an m6, and an M6 above each paw print.

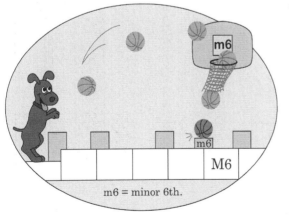

m6 = minor 6th.

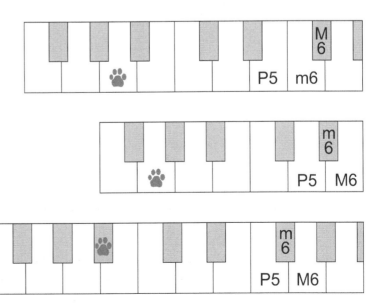

# An M7 is Almost an Octave

Write the note names in the boxes. Use neighboring letters. Draw brackets.
Trace the arrows. Each pair of colored boxes forms a major 7th.

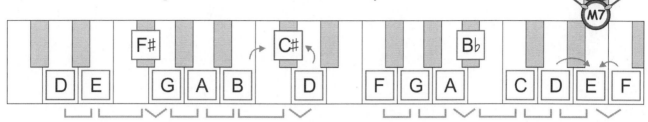

The arrows show that a major 7th is one ___whole___ step larger than a major 6th,

and one ___half___ step smaller than a perfect octave.

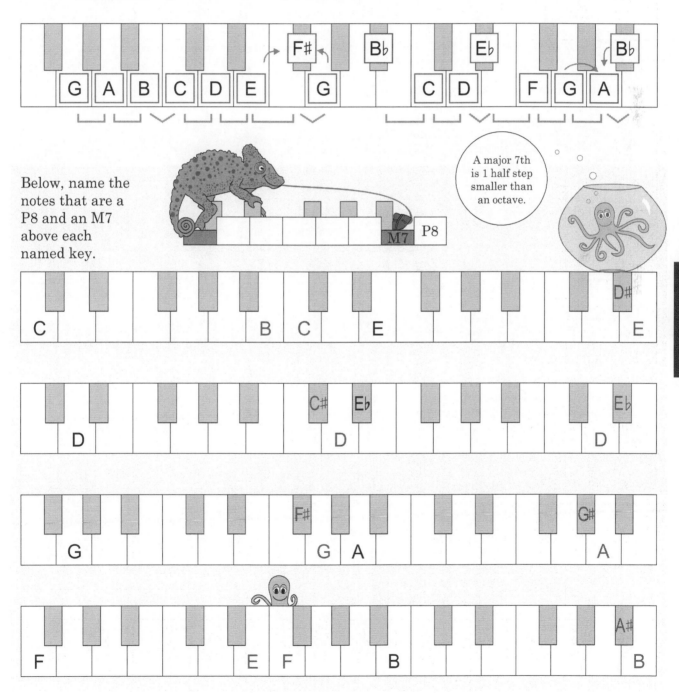

Below, name the notes that are a P8 and an M7 above each named key.

A major 7th is 1 half step smaller than an octave.

2 C

# A Smaller 7th

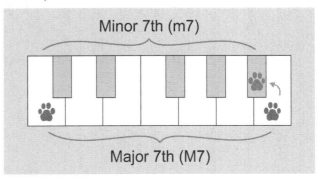

A minor 7th is one half step smaller than a major 7th.

Below, trace the brackets and the arrow.

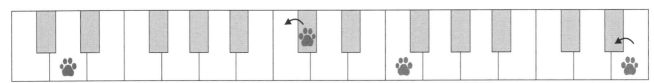

Minor 7th (m7)

Major 7th (M7)

Below, draw an arrow from each right paw print to show a minor 7th.

Next, write the note names in the boxes. Use neighboring letters. Draw brackets. Trace the arrows.

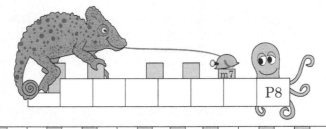

An m7 is 1 whole step smaller than an octave.

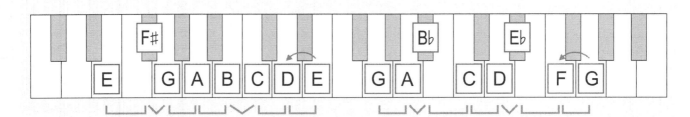

Mark a P8, an M7, and an m7 above each paw print.

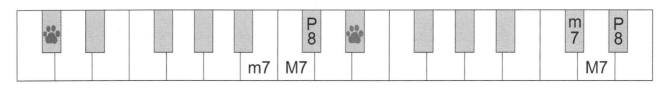

# How to Add Intervals

As you know, we add numbers like this: 2 + 2 = 4.
But intervals are different. They add up in surprising
ways, like this: M2 + M2 = M3. Or m2 + m2 = M2.
Below, write an equation for each pair of intervals.

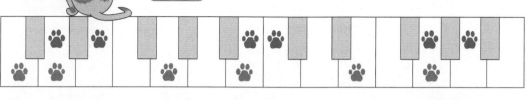

M2 + M2 = M3          M3 + m2 = P4          m3 + M2 = P4

An equation
is a number
sentence
such as 1+1=2.

Before you add two intervals, be sure that the top note of one interval is the bottom note of the other.

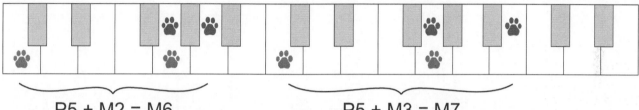

P5 + M2 = M6                    P5 + M3 = M7

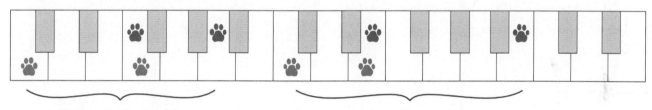

P4 + M3 = M6                    M3 + P5 = M7

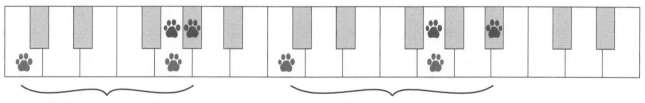

P5 + m2 = m6                    P5 + m3 = m7

Under this keyboard, write an equation for each paw print triad.

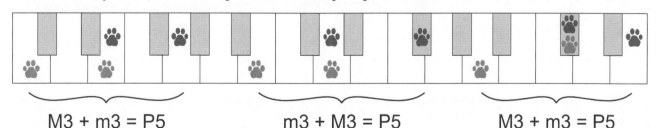

M3 + m3 = P5          m3 + M3 = P5          M3 + m3 = P5

Now you know that M3 + m3 = P__5__.     Also, m3 + M3 = P__5__.

Doctor Mozart Music Theory Workbook, Answers for Level 2 & 3.   © MMVIII, MMXV Machiko and Paul Christopher Musgrave.   Published by April Avenue Music.   www.DoctorMozart.com

# More Inversions

Write an equation for this pair of intervals.

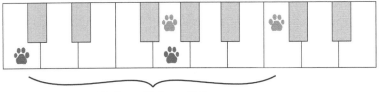

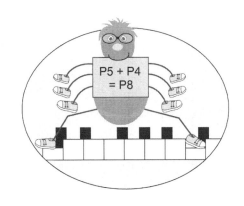

P5 + P4 = P8

Do the above two intervals above add up to a P8? __Yes__ .

An interval and its inversion always add up to one octave. Write equations for these intervals:

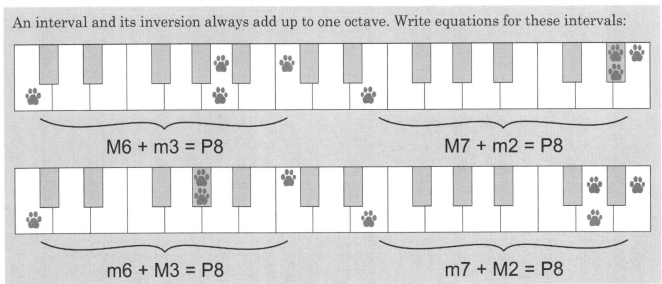

M6 + m3 = P8        M7 + m2 = P8

m6 + M3 = P8        m7 + M2 = P8

The inversion of a *major* interval is always *minor*. The inversion of a *perfect* interval is always *perfect*. Complete these equations:

M6 + _m_ 3 = P8        M3 + _m_ 6 = P8        m2 + _M_ 7 = P8

m6 + _M_ 3 = P8        M7 + _m_ 2 = P8        m7 + _M_ 2 = P8

m3 + _M_ 6 = P8        P5 + _P_ 4 = P8        P4 + _P_ 5 = P8

| Interval | Inversion |
|----------|-----------|
| Major → | Minor |
| Minor → | Major |
| Perfect → | Perfect |

An interval and its inversion are known as complementary intervals.

For each paw print interval, label the notes that form the inversion. Write the equations.

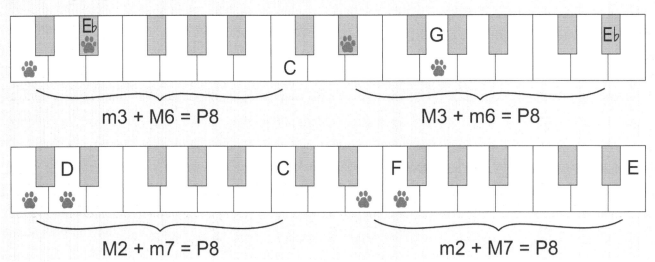

m3 + M6 = P8        M3 + m6 = P8

M2 + m7 = P8        m2 + M7 = P8

Doctor Mozart Music Theory Workbook, Answers for Level 2 & 3.  © MMVIII, MMXV Machiko and Paul Christopher Musgrave.    Published by April Avenue Music.    www.DoctorMozart.com

# Odd and Even Intervals

Some intervals are named with even numbers, such as m2, P4, M6, or P8. The rest are named with odd numbers, such as P1, M3, P5, or m7. Circle the even intervals:

(m2)   P5   (P4)   m3   (m6)

(P8)   P1   m7   (M2)   M3

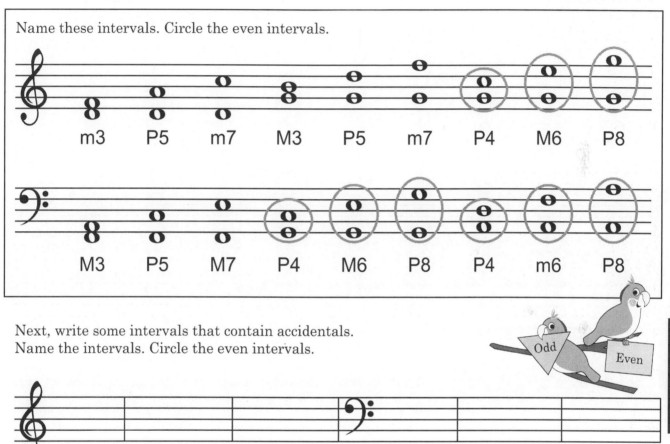

Name these intervals. Circle the even intervals.

m3   P5   m7   M3   P5   m7   P4   M6   P8

M3   P5   M7   P4   M6   P8   P4   m6   P8

Next, write some intervals that contain accidentals.
Name the intervals. Circle the even intervals.

**2 C**

On each staff below, make all the intervals either major or perfect by writing the correct clef and key signature (G major or F major). Name the intervals. Circle the even intervals.

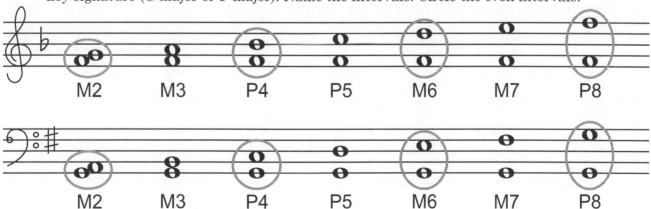

M2   M3   P4   P5   M6   M7   P8

M2   M3   P4   P5   M6   M7   P8

Doctor Mozart Music Theory Workbook, Answers for Level 2 & 3. © MMVIII, MMXV Machiko and Paul Christopher Musgrave. Published by April Avenue Music. www.DoctorMozart.com

# 6th & 7th
# Practice

Label the keys that are a P5, m6, M6, m7, M7, and P8 above each colored key.

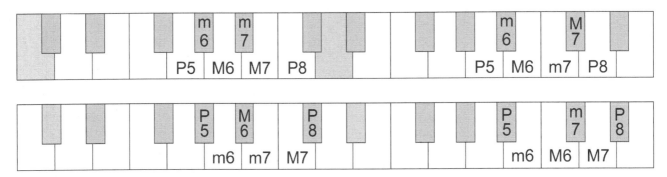

After each given interval, write an interval that has the same bottom note, but is a half step *smaller*. Be sure that the new interval is perfect, major, or minor. Name all the intervals.

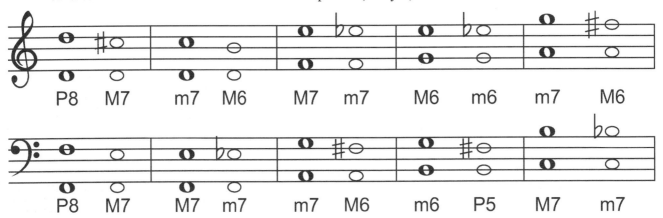

After each given interval, write an interval that has the same bottom note, but is a half step *larger*. Be sure that the new interval is perfect, major, or minor. Name all the intervals.

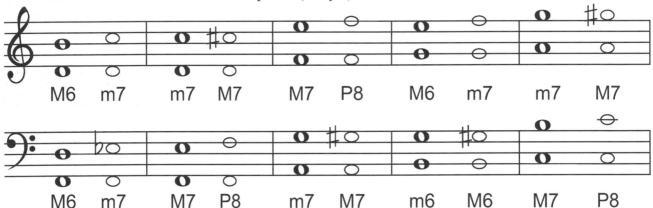

In each bar, write a 6th or 7th, followed by an interval that is one semitone larger.
Name the intervals.

Doctor Mozart Music Theory Workbook, Answers for Level 2 & 3. © MMVIII, MMXV Machiko and Paul Christopher Musgrave. Published by April Avenue Music. www.DoctorMozart.com

# Triad Quiz

major triad!

minor triad!

On the keyboards below, an invisible alien played some triads. She marked the 3rd of each triad with a letter M for major, or m for minor. Write the missing notes for each triad. Name each triad.

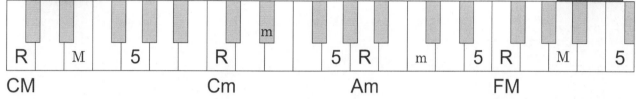

CM      Cm      Am      FM

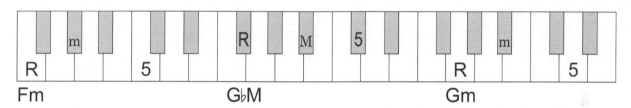

Fm      GbM      Gm

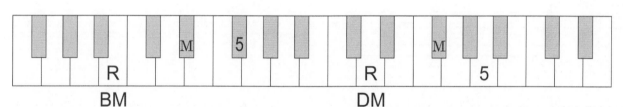

BM      DM

Next, each printed note is the 3rd of a triad. Write the triads indicated. Name them.

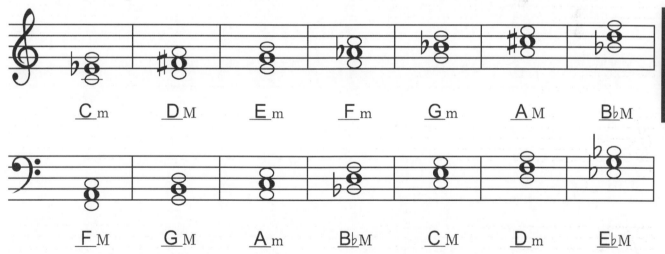

Cm    DM    Em    Fm    Gm    AM    BbM

FM    GM    Am    BbM    CM    Dm    EbM

**2 C**

Next, each printed note is the 5th of a triad. Write the triads indicated. Name them.

Cm    CM    AM    Am      Gm    GM    DM    Dm

Doctor Mozart Music Theory Workbook, Answers for Level 2 & 3.  © MMVIII, MMXV  Machiko and Paul Christopher Musgrave.    Published by April Avenue Music.    www.DoctorMozart.com

# Harmonic Minor Scales

In harmonic minor scales, always write an accidental such as ♯ or ♮ to raise the leading note.

The A *natural* minor scale has no accidentals.

Trace the bracket.

I   II   III   IV   V   VI   VII   I

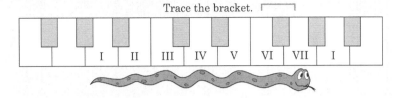

The A **harmonic** minor scale has a raised leading note.

Trace the brackets.

I   II   III   IV   V   VI   VII   I

Since the 7th note is raised, it is more than a whole step away from the 6th note of the scale. That's why there are *two* brackets – a square *and* a V – between those notes.

Next, write the key signatures and ascending scales indicated. Draw lines.

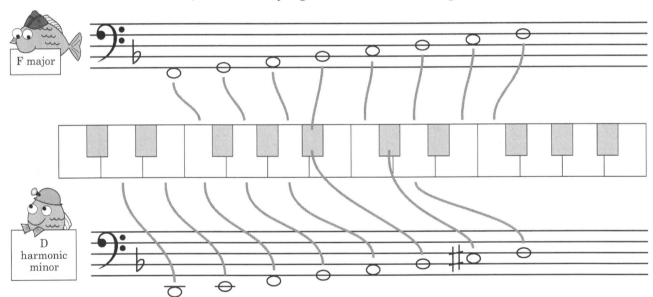

F major

D harmonic minor

Convert each natural minor scale to a harmonic minor scale by raising the leading note. Draw square and V brackets.

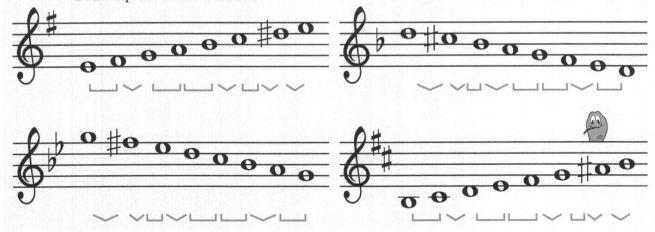

# Test Your Relatives

On each staff, write the key signature and ascending scale. Draw square and V brackets. Draw lines to the keyboard.

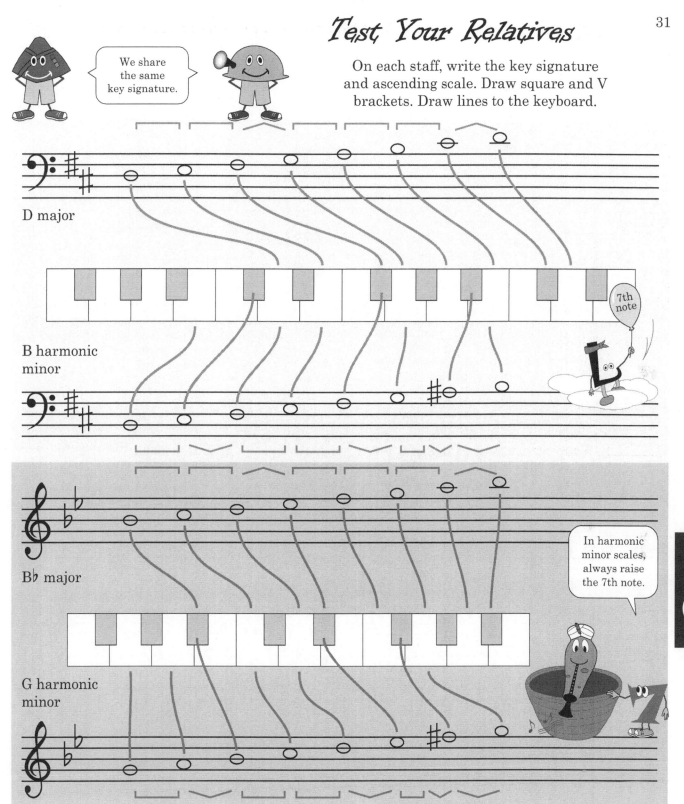

We share the same key signature.

D major

7th note

B harmonic minor

Bb major

In harmonic minor scales, always raise the 7th note.

2 C

G harmonic minor

Write the correct clefs. Name each key signature two ways: As a major key, and as its relative minor.

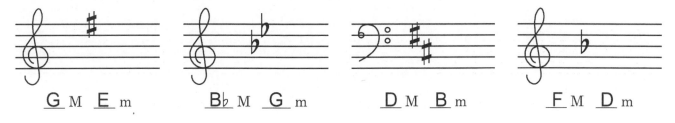

G M  E m     Bb M  G m     D M  B m     F M  D m

Doctor Mozart Music Theory Workbook, Answers for Level 2 & 3.  © MMVIII, MMXV Machiko and Paul Christopher Musgrave.     Published by April Avenue Music.     www.DoctorMozart.com

# Primary Triads in Harmonic Minor Scales

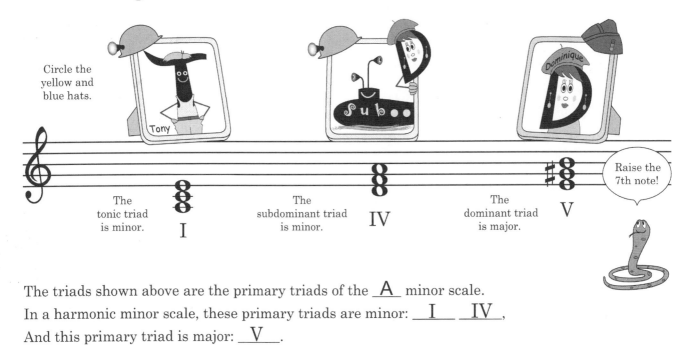

Circle the yellow and blue hats.

The tonic triad is minor. I

The subdominant triad is minor. IV

The dominant triad is major. V

Raise the 7th note!

The triads shown above are the primary triads of the __A__ minor scale.

In a harmonic minor scale, these primary triads are minor: __I__ __IV__ ,

And this primary triad is major: __V__ .

Next, write the key signatures, harmonic minor scales, and primary triads. Number the notes. Name each primary triad. For example, Gm = G minor triad. Use M for major and m for minor.

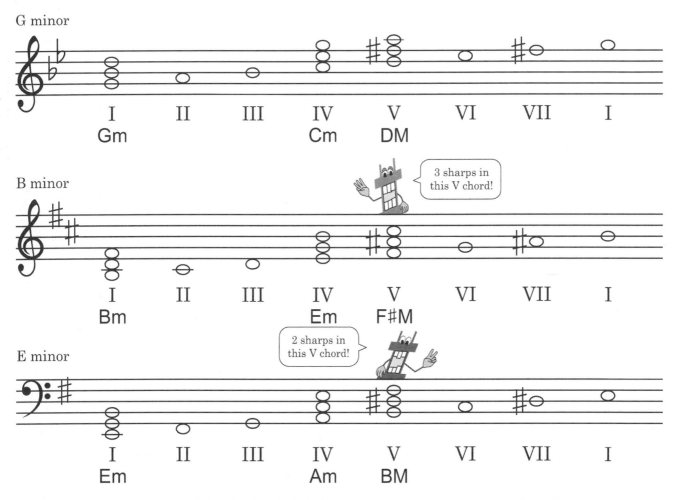

G minor

| I | II | III | IV | V | VI | VII | I |
| Gm | | | Cm | DM | | | |

B minor

3 sharps in this V chord!

| I | II | III | IV | V | VI | VII | I |
| Bm | | | Em | F#M | | | |

2 sharps in this V chord!

E minor

| I | II | III | IV | V | VI | VII | I |
| Em | | | Am | BM | | | |

# How Long Are Dotted Quarter Notes?

Answer with a single note.

Tap this rhythm several times until you can do it well.

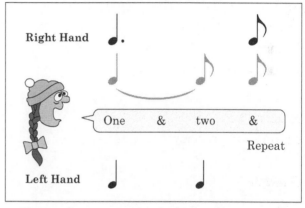

The top notes have the same rhythm as the gray notes.

**2**
**C**

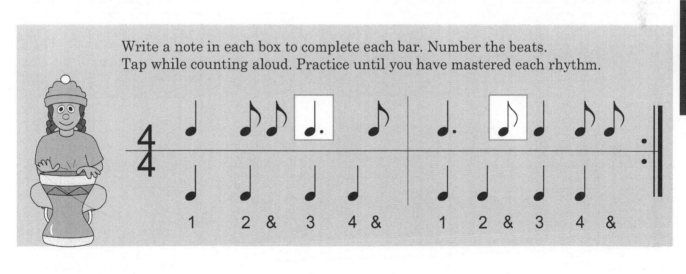

Write a note in each box to complete each bar. Number the beats.
Tap while counting aloud. Practice until you have mastered each rhythm.

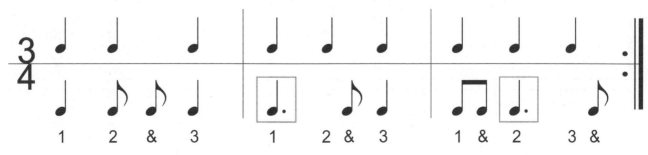

Doctor Mozart Music Theory Workbook, Answers for Level 2 & 3.  © MMVIII, MMXV  Machiko and Paul Christopher Musgrave.   Published by April Avenue Music.   www.DoctorMozart.com

# Sixteenth Notes

A 16th note has two flags.
Here is how to draw a 16th note.

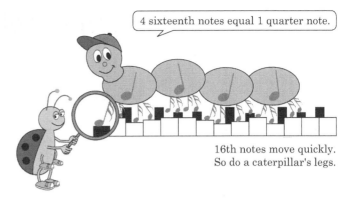

16th notes move quickly.
So do a caterpillar's legs.

 Trace these notes.

Two sixteenth notes are as
long as __1__ eighth note.

Four sixteenth notes are as
long as __1__ quarter note.

Trace these notes.

For easier reading, adjacent 16th
notes can be connected with beams.

Flags                    Beams

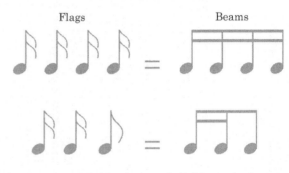

Connect 16th notes with a beam only if they are in the same beat.

Next, change the flags to beams. Change the beams to flags. Draw bar lines. Tap the rhythm.

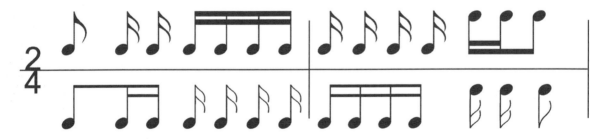

Write a single note to complete each equation.

# Sixteenth Rests

This is a sixteenth rest.
It tells you to stay silent
for the length
of a sixteenth note.

How to draw a 16th rest

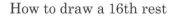

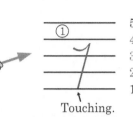

Fill these two bars with
sixteenth and eighth rests.
Count the beats.

1 - po - ta - to

Draw bar lines.

Answer with one rest.

Write a single rest in each box to make the total duration in each box one quarter note.

2 C

# 8th and 16th Notes and Rests

Write *rests* to ensure that the total duration in each box is one quarter note.

Write *notes* to ensure that the total duration in each box is one quarter note.

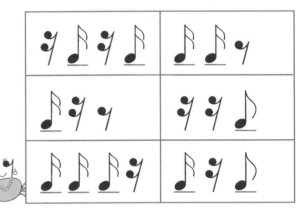

Complete each equation with a single rest.

Next, write the correct clefs. Name each key signature as a minor key. Fill the bars with 8th and 16th notes and rests. Number the beats. Use an accidental to raise each leading note.

B minor

G minor

Doctor Mozart Music Theory Workbook, Answers for Level 2 & 3. © MMVIII, MMXV Machiko and Paul Christopher Musgrave.    Published by April Avenue Music.    www.DoctorMozart.com

# Scale Review

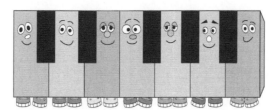

On each staff, write the correct key signature. Write a descending scale and the primary triads. Draw square and V brackets.

Bb Major

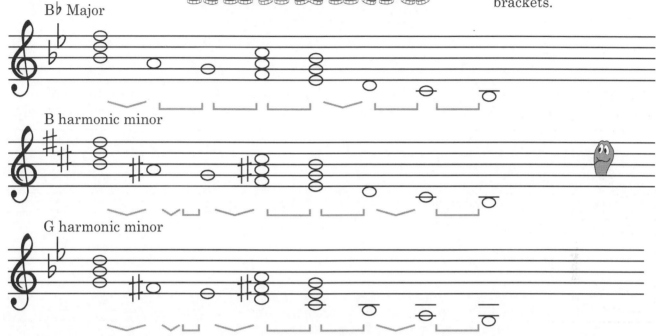

B harmonic minor

G harmonic minor

Name this scale. Circle any notes that do not belong in the G major scale.

D major

Name this scale. Circle any notes that do not belong in the D major scale.

B harmonic minor

Name this scale. Circle any notes that do not belong in the G major scale.

E harmonic minor

Name this scale. Circle any notes that do not belong in the E harmonic minor scale.

G major

Name this scale. Circle any notes that do not belong in the F major scale.

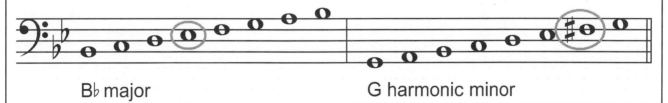

Bb major

Name this scale. Circle any notes that do not belong in the B flat major scale.

G harmonic minor

2
C

# Chord Quiz

Each printed note is the tonic
of a harmonic minor scale.
Write the key signatures.
Write the primary triads.

Primary Triads

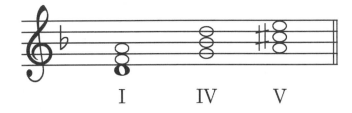

I       IV       V

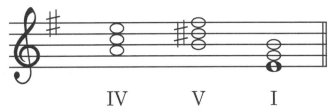

IV       V       I

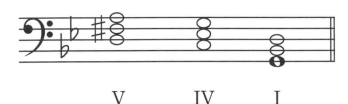

V       IV       I

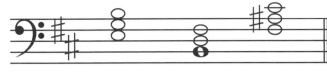

IV       I       V

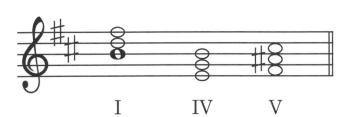

I       IV       V

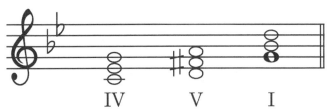

IV       V       I

Chords & keys.

Next, some of these triads belong to more than one scale.
Under each triad, write a Roman numeral to indicate the
triad's position in each scale. If it does not belong, write an X.

| | | | | | | | |
|---|---|---|---|---|---|---|---|
| C major scale | IV | V | I | X | X | X | X |
| G major scale | X | I | IV | X | V | X | X |
| D major scale | X | IV | X | X | I | V | X |
| F major scale | I | X | V | IV | X | X | X |
| B flat major scale | V | X | X | I | X | X | IV |

Doctor Mozart Music Theory Workbook, Answers for Level 2 & 3.  © MMVIII, MMXV  Machiko and Paul Christopher Musgrave.    Published by April Avenue Music.    www.DoctorMozart.com

# Doctor Mozart® Music Theory Workbook

## In-Depth Piano Theory Fun for Children's Music Lessons and Home Schooling

### Level 3 - Contents

Every day, start by reviewing what you learned the day before. Then complete a page or two, and you will make good progress.

Highly effective for beginners learning a musical instrument.

Hi! I'm Doctor Mozart.

Doctor Mozart workbooks are filled with friendly cartoon characters. They make it fun to learn music theory in-depth. And in-depth music theory knowledge is essential for children learning a musical instrument. Use Doctor Mozart workbooks by themselves or with other teaching materials. Use them for music lessons and for home schooling.

The authors, Machiko and Paul Musgrave, are both graduates of Juilliard. Machiko has taught piano and theory at Soai University in Japan. Paul is an Associate of the Royal Conservatory of Music. The authors hope you enjoy using this book!

3

**Copyright laws protect the right of authors and publishers to earn a living from their work. Please respect these laws, and pay for the books you use and enjoy. Photocopying or reproducing this book in any manner may lead to prosecution.**

Many thanks to Kevin Musgrave for his meticulous proof-reading and insightful suggestions.
Created by Machiko and Paul Christopher Musgrave. Illustrated by Machiko Yamane Musgrave.
Version 1.0.1

# How Long Are Dotted Eighth Notes?

The dot makes the note longer.

Below, draw a line to connect the notes that have the same duration.

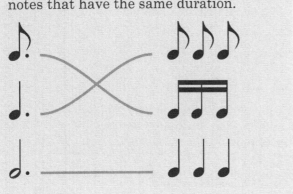

Draw a line to connect each *dot* with a note that has the same duration.

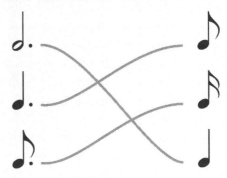

Re-write the rhythm below. Change the flags to beams. Change the beams to flags. Notice how a beam can connect a dotted eighth note and a 16th note.

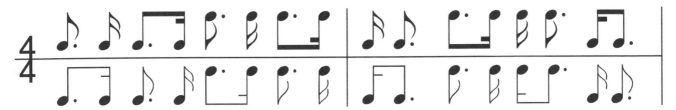

Fill these bars with notes. Include some dotted eighth notes. Number the beats.

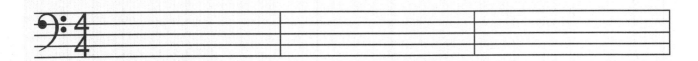

Tap this rhythm, hands together. Repeat until perfect. Then switch hands.

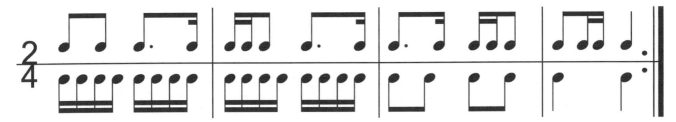

Doctor Mozart Music Theory Workbook, Answers for Level 2 & 3.  © MMVIII, MMXV  Machiko and Paul Christopher Musgrave.    Published by April Avenue Music.    www.DoctorMozart.com

# 4 is Common, 2 is Cut

**C = 4/4**

This sign looks like a C. It's another way of writing a 4/4 time signature. The C stands for *common time*.

**₵ = 2/2**

This C with a line through it means cut time, or **alla breve**. It tells you there are 2 half note beats in each bar.

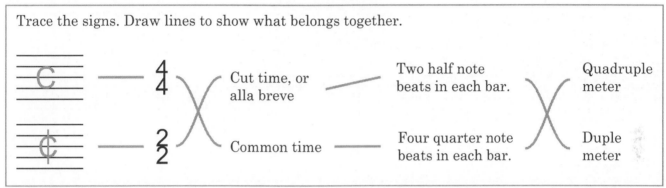

Trace the signs. Draw lines to show what belongs together.

Number the beats. Draw bar lines. Tap the beats while counting aloud.

Complete each equation with a single rest.

Doctor Mozart Music Theory Workbook, Answers for Level 2 & 3. © MMVIII, MMXV Machiko and Paul Christopher Musgrave. Published by April Avenue Music. www.DoctorMozart.com

# Major Scale Review

Write these major scales, descending only.
Use accidentals, not key signatures.
Draw a square bracket at each whole step.
Draw a V bracket at each half step. Then write
each key signature after the double bar line.

A key is the set of notes
you would use to play a scale.

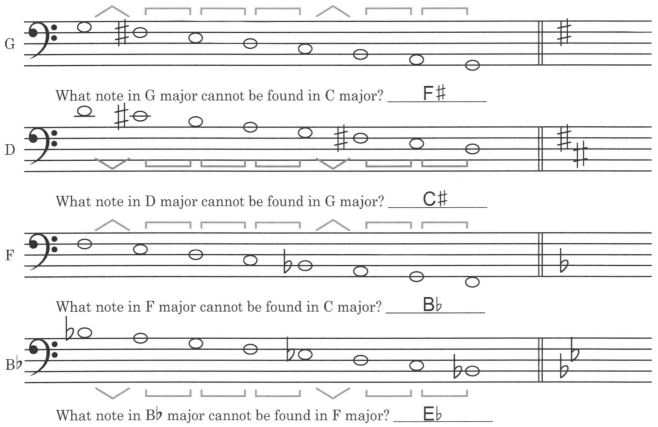

What note in G major cannot be found in C major? __F#__

What note in D major cannot be found in G major? __C#__

What note in F major cannot be found in C major? __B♭__

What note in B♭ major cannot be found in F major? __E♭__

Write the correct clef before each key signature. Name each key signature as a major key.

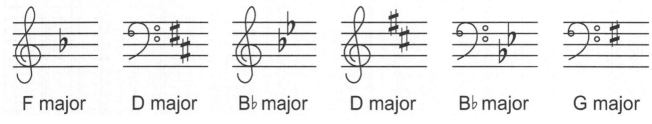

**F major**   **D major**   **B♭ major**   **D major**   **B♭ major**   **G major**

Next, write the correct key signatures. Write the major and relative minor tonic notes.

F major          G major          D major          B♭ major

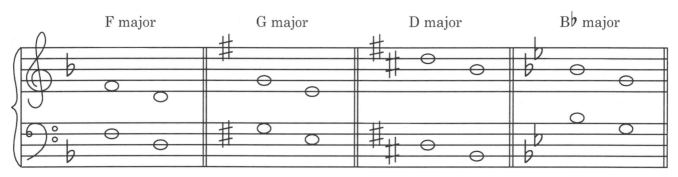

Doctor Mozart Music Theory Workbook, Answers for Level 2 & 3.   © MMVIII, MMXV  Machiko and Paul Christopher Musgrave.   Published by April Avenue Music.   www.DoctorMozart.com

# Sharp 4ths & 5ths

Review

These intervals are used in key signatures.

Name the intervals between these notes.

P4  P5  P4  P4    P4  P5  P4  P4

Name these intervals. Draw lines to the keys.

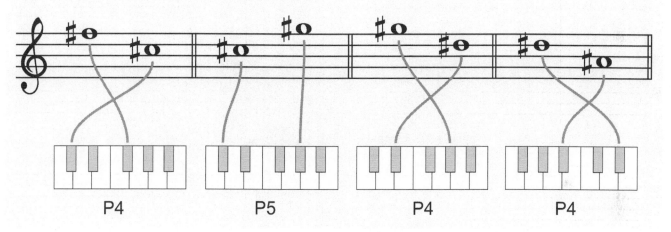

P4    P5    P4    P4

Next, write these intervals on the staff. Follow the direction of the arrows.

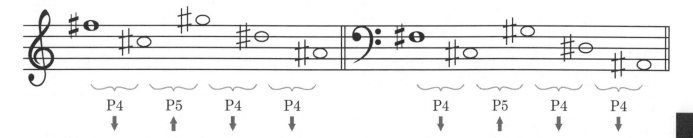

P4  P5  P4  P4    P4  P5  P4  P4

Name the intervals between these sharps.

P4  P5  P4  P4    P4  P5  P4  P4

3

Doctor Mozart Music Theory Workbook, Answers for Level 2 & 3.  © MMVIII, MMXV  Machiko and Paul Christopher Musgrave.   Published by April Avenue Music.   www.DoctorMozart.com

# Sharp Key Signatures

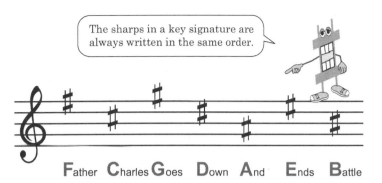

The sharps in a key signature are always written in the same order.

Father Charles
Goes Down
And Ends Battle.

The sentence above will help you remember the correct order for sharps in key signatures.

Circle the words that match the sharps in each key signature.

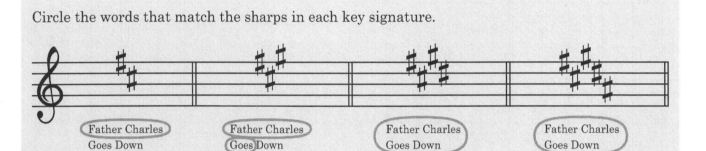

In every sharp key signature, the last sharp is for the leading note of the major scale.

Below, write the words that help you remember the sharps in each key signature. Then write the leading note and the tonic on the staff.

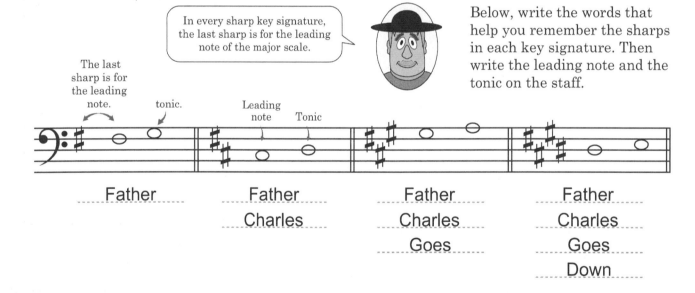

Trace these key signatures. Circle the words that match the sharps.
Write the leading note and tonic.

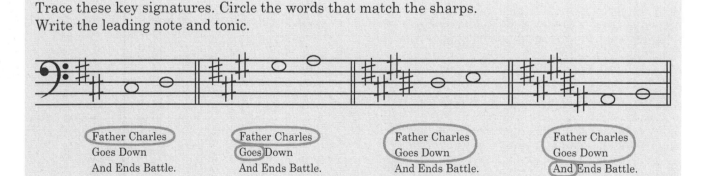

Doctor Mozart Music Theory Workbook, Answers for Level 2 & 3.  © MMVIII, MMXV Machiko and Paul Christopher Musgrave.  Published by April Avenue Music.  www.DoctorMozart.com

# The A Major Scale

The Roman numerals on this keyboard show the A major scale.
Draw square and V brackets. Which notes are sharp?  F♯  C♯  G♯

The A major
scale has
3 sharps.

Father
Charles Goes

The Roman numerals
are printed in black
and gray to show the
2 tetrachords.

Each tetrachord
spans a P4.

III    VI  VII
I  II    IV  V    I

Tetrachord   Whole step   Tetrachord

Next, write the primary triads (I, IV and V). Draw square and V brackets.
Draw lines from the scale notes to the keyboard.

The A major key
signature has
an F♯, a C♯
and a G♯.

Tonic    Sub-
dominant Dominant

Write the words that help
you remember these sharps.

Father Charles Goes

On the staff below, write an F♯ minor key signature. Write an
ascending F♯ harmonic minor scale. Write the primary triads.
Draw lines from the scale notes to the keyboard.

Raise the
7th note.

F♯ minor is the
relative minor
of A major. So
both scales have
the same key
signature.

3

Major

Doctor Mozart Music Theory Workbook, Answers for Level 2 & 3.   © MMVIII, MMXV Machiko and Paul Christopher Musgrave.   Published by April Avenue Music.   www.DoctorMozart.com

# The E Major Scale

Here is an E major scale. Draw brackets. Which notes are sharp?  F#  C#  G#  D#

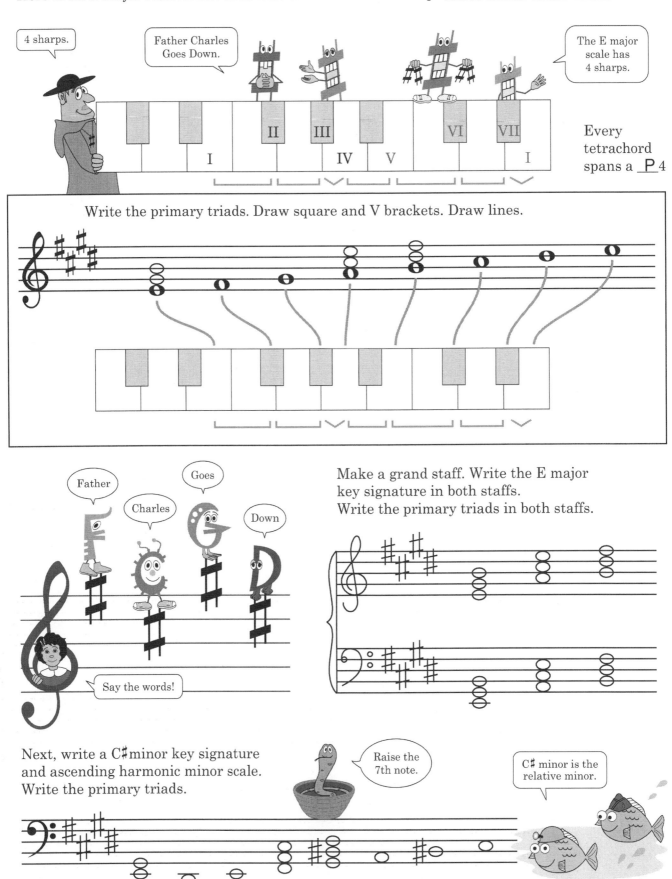

Make a grand staff. Write the E major
key signature in both staffs.
Write the primary triads in both staffs.

Next, write a C# minor key signature
and ascending harmonic minor scale.
Write the primary triads.

# The B Major Scale

Here is a B major scale. Draw brackets. Which notes are sharp?  F#  C#  G#  D#  A#

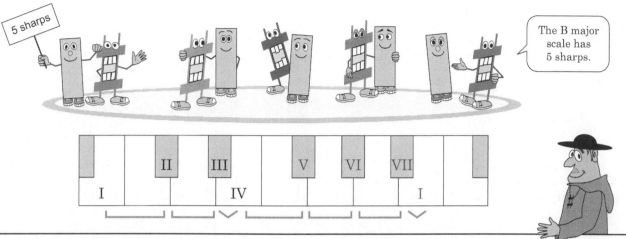

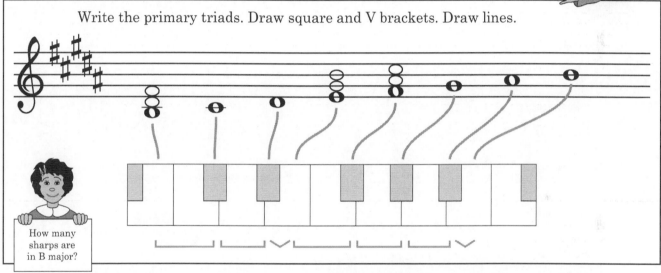

Write the primary triads. Draw square and V brackets. Draw lines.

How many sharps are in B major?

___5___

Make a grand staff. Write the B major key signature in both staffs.
Write the primary triads in both staffs.

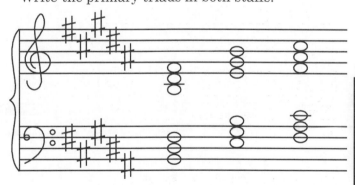

**3**

For each key signature, write the correct clef. Write the major and relative minor tonic notes.

Doctor Mozart Music Theory Workbook, Answers for Level 2 & 3.  © MMVIII, MMXV  Machiko and Paul Christopher Musgrave.    Published by April Avenue Music.    www.DoctorMozart.com

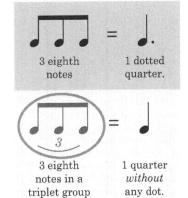

# Triplets

3 eighth notes = 1 dotted quarter.

3 eighth notes in a triplet group = 1 quarter *without* any dot.

Circle the triplet group at left.
It has a numeral 3 with a slur.

1 eighth note triplet group = __1__ quarter note.
3 eighth notes = __1__ dotted __quarter__ note.

Below, add a slur to each triplet group.
Tap hands together. Switch hands.

Sometimes triplets are written without a slur.

Sixteenth notes and quarter notes can be triplets too.
Write a single note to complete each equation.

Draw a line from each group of notes to the matching single note.

Number the beats. Draw bar lines. Tap while counting aloud. Repeat until perfect.

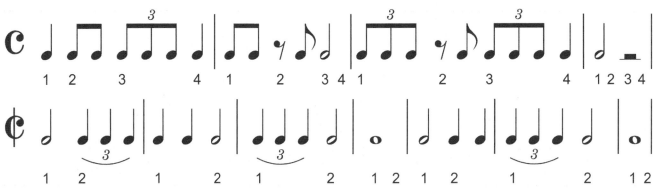

Doctor Mozart Music Theory Workbook, Answers for Level 2 & 3.  © MMVIII, MMXV  Machiko and Paul Christopher Musgrave.  Published by April Avenue Music.  www.DoctorMozart.com

# Piglet Triplets

Complete each time signature.
Tap hands together. Repeat until
perfect. Then switch hands.

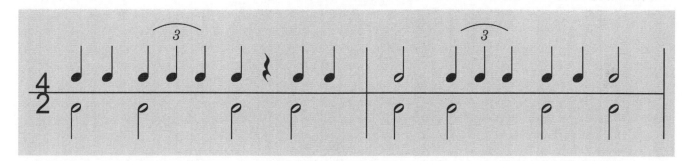

Number the beats. Draw bar lines. Tap while counting aloud. Repeat until perfect.

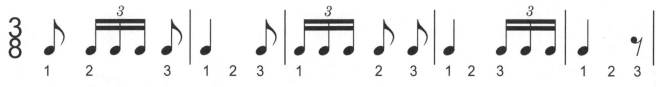

Complete each equation by writing a single triplet group.

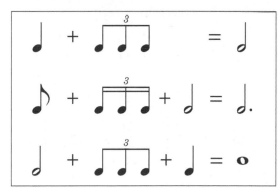

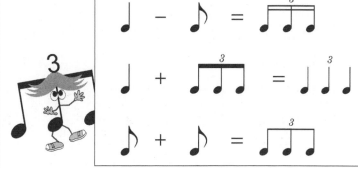

Doctor Mozart Music Theory Workbook, Answers for Level 2 & 3. © MMVIII, MMXV Machiko and Paul Christopher Musgrave. Published by April Avenue Music. www.DoctorMozart.com

12

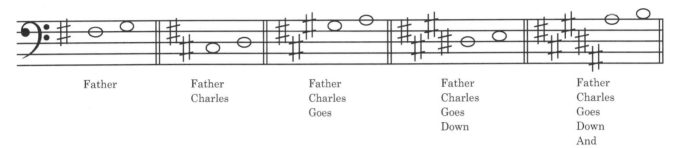

Write the key signatures that match the words. Write the leading note and the tonic for each.

Father

Father
Charles

Father
Charles
Goes

Father
Charles
Goes
Down

Father
Charles
Goes
Down
And

Next, each printed note is the tonic of a major scale. Write the key signatures. Name them. Write the leading notes. Write the words that help you remember the sharps.

A major  E major  D major  B major

Father
Charles
Goes

Father
Charles
Goes
Down

Father
Charles

Father
Charles
Goes
Down
And

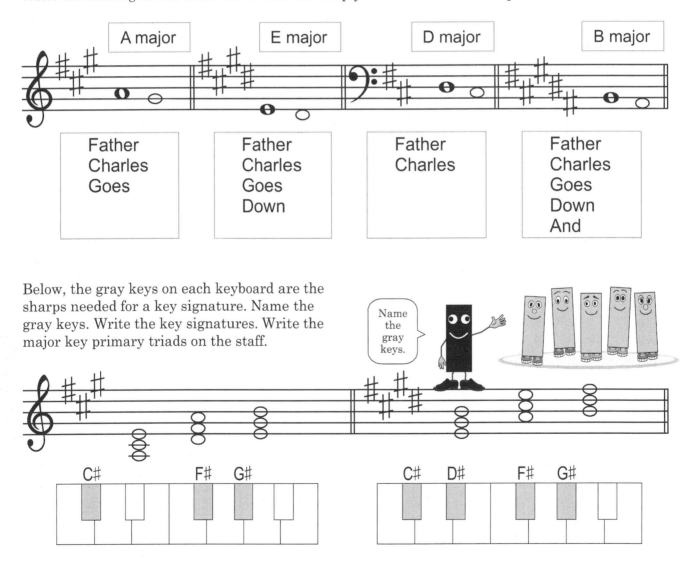

Below, the gray keys on each keyboard are the sharps needed for a key signature. Name the gray keys. Write the key signatures. Write the major key primary triads on the staff.

Name the gray keys.

C#  F#  G#

C#  D#  F#  G#

# Flat 4ths & 5ths

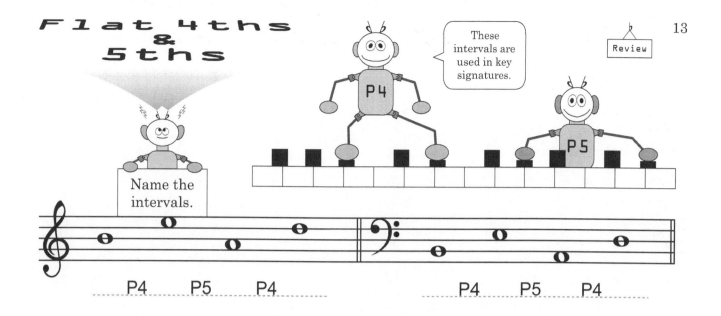

These intervals are used in key signatures.

P4   P5

Review

Name the intervals.

P4    P5    P4          P4    P5    P4

Name these intervals. Draw lines to the keys.

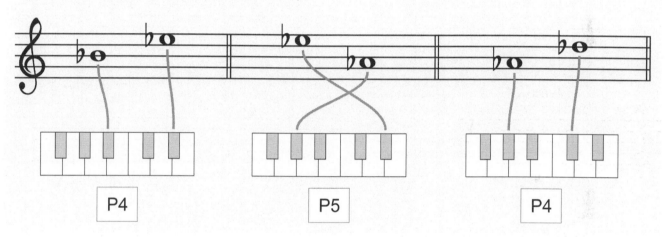

P4          P5          P4

Write these intervals. Follow the direction of the arrows.

P4     P5     P4          P4     P5     P4

3

Name the intervals between these flats.

P4  P5  P4          P4  P5  P4

Doctor Mozart Music Theory Workbook, Answers for Level 2 & 3.   © MMVIII, MMXV  Machiko and Paul Christopher Musgrave.   Published by April Avenue Music.   www.DoctorMozart.com

# Flat Key Signatures

Battle Ends And Down Goes Charles' Father.

The sentence above will help you remember the correct order for flats in key signatures.

Battle Ends And Down Goes Charles' Father

Circle the words that match the flats in each key signature.

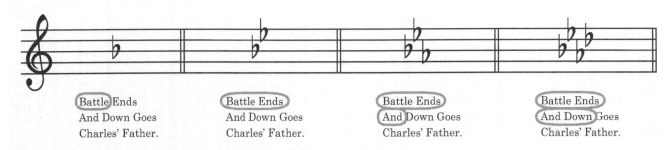

Battle Ends
And Down Goes
Charles' Father.

Battle Ends
And Down Goes
Charles' Father.

Battle Ends
And Down Goes
Charles' Father.

Battle Ends
And Down Goes
Charles' Father.

Below, write the words that help you remember the flats in each key signature. Circle the 2nd last flat. Write the major and relative minor tonic notes.

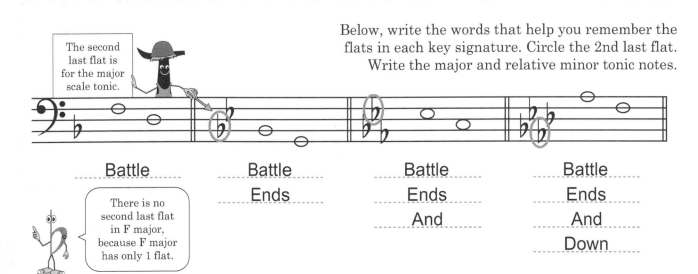

Battle

Battle
Ends

Battle
Ends
And

Battle
Ends
And
Down

Trace these key signatures. Circle the words that match the flats. Circle the 2nd last flat. Write the major and relative minor tonic notes.

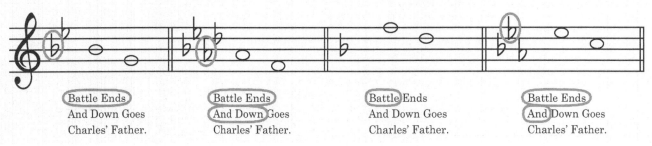

Battle Ends
And Down Goes
Charles' Father.

Battle Ends
And Down Goes
Charles' Father.

Battle Ends
And Down Goes
Charles' Father.

Battle Ends
And Down Goes
Charles' Father.

Doctor Mozart Music Theory Workbook, Answers for Level 2 & 3. © MMVIII, MMXV Machiko and Paul Christopher Musgrave.    Published by April Avenue Music.    www.DoctorMozart.com

# E♭ Major Scale

Here is an E flat major scale. Draw brackets. Which notes are flat?  B♭  E♭  A♭

Circle the second last flat. It is for the major scale __tonic__ note.
Write the primary triads. Draw square and V brackets. Draw lines.

On the staff below, write a C minor key signature. Write an ascending C harmonic minor scale.
Write the primary triads. Draw lines from the scale notes to the keyboard.

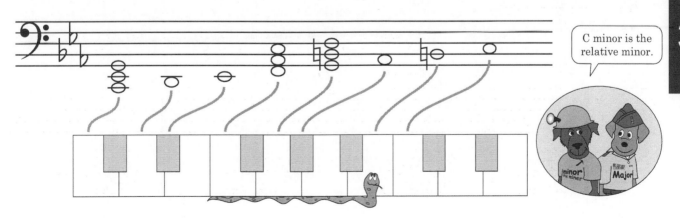

# A♭ Major Scale

Here is an A flat major scale. Draw brackets.
Which notes are flat?  __B♭__  __E♭__  __A♭__  __D♭__

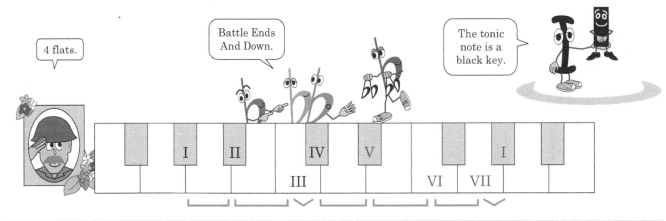

4 flats.

Battle Ends And Down.

The tonic note is a black key.

Circle the 2nd last flat. Write the primary triads. Draw square and V brackets. Draw lines.

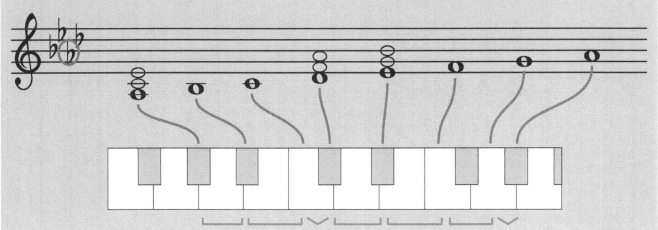

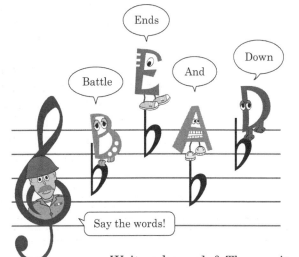

Ends

And

Down

Battle

Say the words!

Make a grand staff. Write the A flat major key signature in both staffs. Write the primary triads in both staffs.

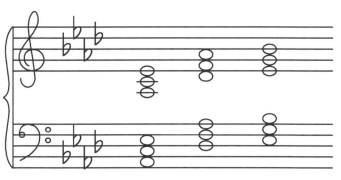

Write a bass clef. Then write an F minor key signature and ascending harmonic minor scale. Write the primary triads.

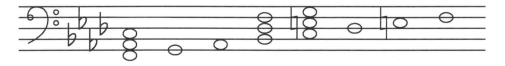

F minor is the relative minor.

Doctor Mozart Music Theory Workbook, Answers for Level 2 & 3.  © MMVIII, MMXV Machiko and Paul Christopher Musgrave.   Published by April Avenue Music.   www.DoctorMozart.com

# Flat Key Signature Quiz

The second last flat is for the __tonic__ note of the major scale. Here, write the key signatures that match the words. Write 2 tonic notes: One for the major scale, and one for the relative minor.

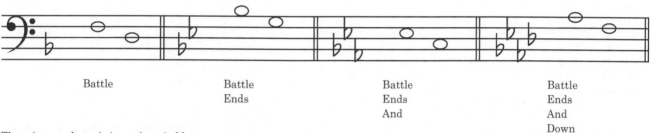

| Battle | Battle Ends | Battle Ends And | Battle Ends And Down |

The minor scale tonic is a minor 3rd lower.

Next, write these major key signatures. Write the words that help you remember the flats. Write two tonic notes: One for the major scale, and one for the relative minor.

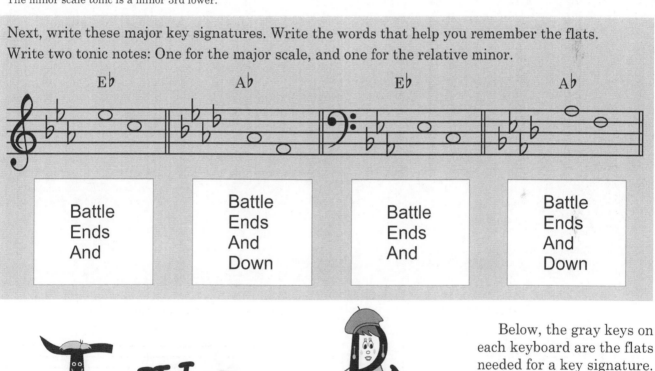

Battle Ends And

Battle Ends And Down

Battle Ends And

Battle Ends And Down

Below, the gray keys on each keyboard are the flats needed for a key signature. Name the gray keys. Write the key signatures. Write the major key primary triads.

**3**

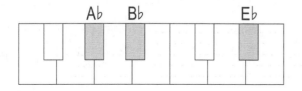

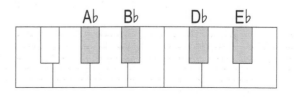

Doctor Mozart Music Theory Workbook, Answers for Level 2 & 3. © MMVIII, MMXV Machiko and Paul Christopher Musgrave. Published by April Avenue Music. www.DoctorMozart.com

# Compound Time Signatures

For each of these time signatures, circle the number that tells you how many beats are in each bar.

　⑥/8　　⑨/8　　⑫/8

You can tell these are compound time signatures, because each has 6, 9, or 12 on top. Compound time signatures always have __6__, __9__, or __12__ on top. The beats are divided into groups of 3.

Below, number the beats. Trace the accents.

In compound time, the beats are in groups of 3, but the groups are not triplets.

Next, complete each time signature. Write compound, duple, triple, or quadruple. Number the beats.

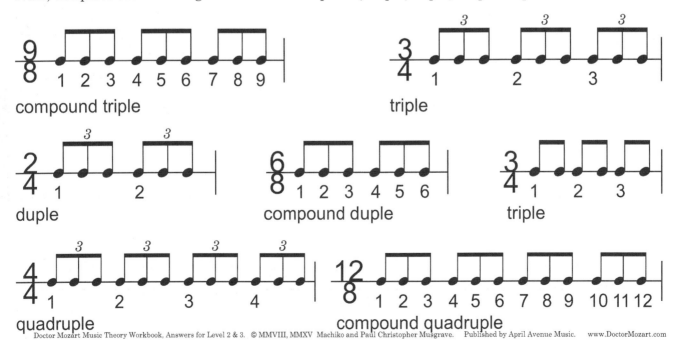

Doctor Mozart Music Theory Workbook, Answers for Level 2 & 3.　© MMVIII, MMXV Machiko and Paul Christopher Musgrave.　Published by April Avenue Music.　www.DoctorMozart.com

# Compound Time Quiz

Complete these two time signatures.
Tap the rhythms, hands together.
Repeat until perfect. Then switch hands.

Write the correct note in each box to complete each bar. Number the beats.

1 2 3  4  5 6  1 2 3  4 5 6  1 2 3  4  5 6  1  2  3  4 5 6

1  2 3 4 5 6  1 2 3  4  5 6  1  2  3  4 5 6

In compound time, the beats are in groups of __3__,
but the groups are not __triplets__.

Watch for triplets.

Write the correct time signature at each arrow.

# Relative Major & Minor Scale Quiz

Label the notes in each scale. Draw a line between each pair of keyboards to show which notes are different. Write I, IV and V.

 = major    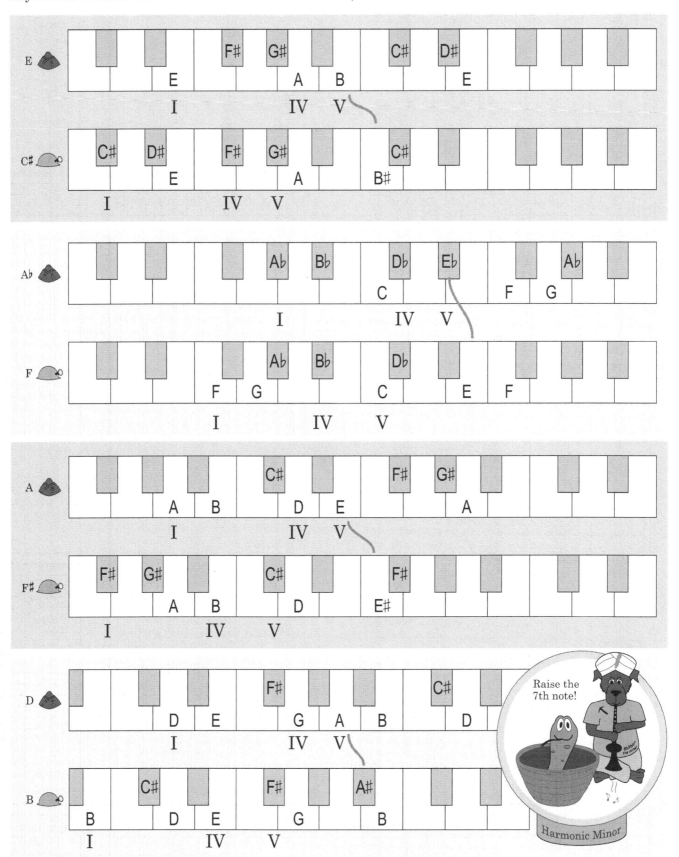 = harmonic minor

# Melodic Minor Scales

A melodic minor scale sounds different going up than it does going down. The 6th and 7th notes are the ones that change.

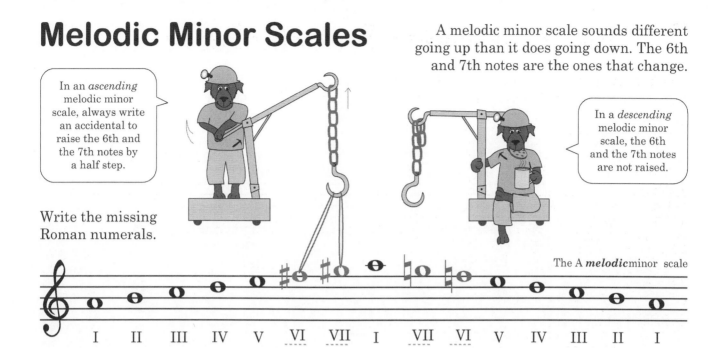

In an *ascending* melodic minor scale, always write an accidental to raise the 6th and the 7th notes by a half step.

In a *descending* melodic minor scale, the 6th and the 7th notes are not raised.

Write the missing Roman numerals.

The A *melodic* minor scale

I  II  III  IV  V  VI  VII  I  VII  VI  V  IV  III  II  I

Name the raised notes in the ascending form of this A melodic minor scale: __F#__ and __G#__

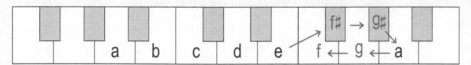

A descending melodic minor scale is the same as a descending natural minor scale.

Higher on the way up.

Below, write accidentals to convert these natural minor scales into melodic minor scales.

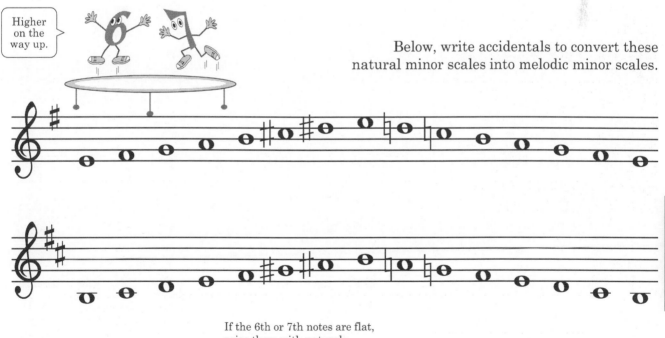

If the 6th or 7th notes are flat, raise them with naturals.

3

Doctor Mozart Music Theory Workbook, Answers for Level 2 & 3.   © MMVIII, MMXV  Machiko and Paul Christopher Musgrave.    Published by April Avenue Music.    www.DoctorMozart.com

# Relative Minor Scale Quiz

Write the key signatures. Write each scale
on the staff, ascending and descending.
Write the scale notes on the keyboards.

E flat major scale.

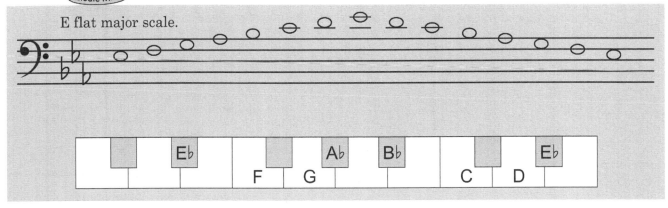

C natural minor scale.

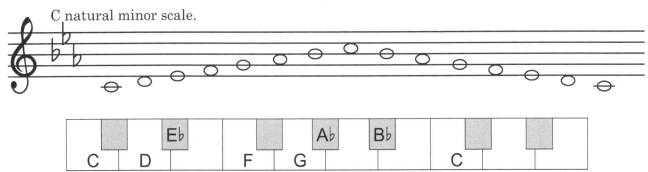

C harmonic minor scale.

Always write an accidental to raise the
7th note of a harmonic minor scale.

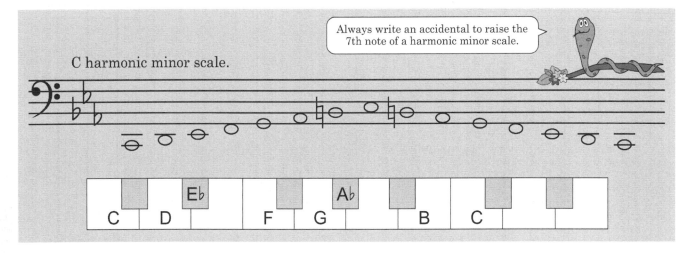

C melodic minor scale.

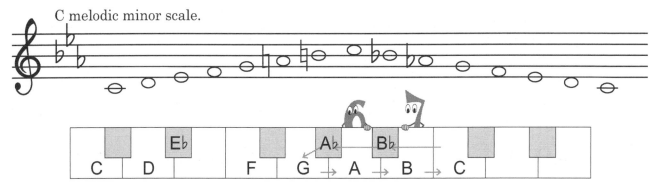

Doctor Mozart Music Theory Workbook, Answers for Level 2 & 3. © MMVIII, MMXV  Machiko and Paul Christopher Musgrave.     Published by April Avenue Music.     www.DoctorMozart.com

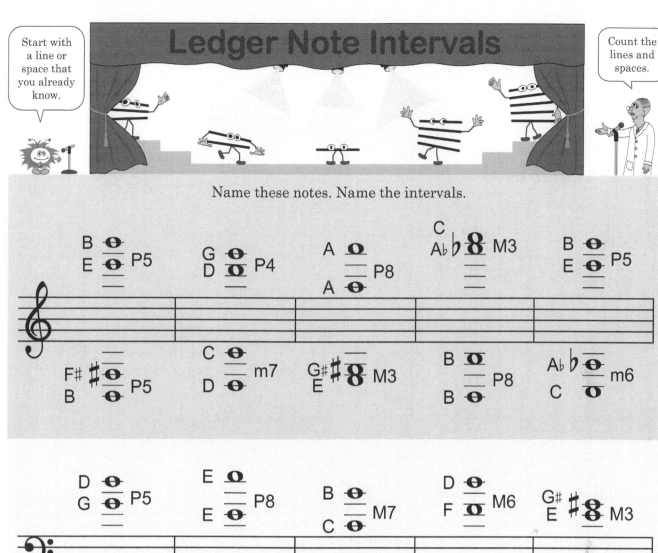

# Ledger Note Intervals

Start with a line or space that you already know.

Count the lines and spaces.

Name these notes. Name the intervals.

Treble clef staff:

B / E — P5    G / D — P4    A / A — P8    C / Ab ♭ — M3    B / E — P5

F# / B — P5    C / D — m7    G# / E — M3    B / B — P8    Ab / C — m6

Bass clef staff:

D / G — P5    E / E — P8    B / C — M7    D / F — M6    G# / E — M3

A / D — P5    C# / D — M7    B / E — P5    C / C — P8    D / F — M6

# Pedal Terminology

Una corda means use the left pedal.

Use the left pedal to play the piano more quietly. Una corda means *one string*.

una corda

Tre corde means release the left pedal.

Release the left pedal to play the piano at a normal or loud volume. Tre corde means *three strings*.

tre corde

# Ledger Note Exercise

Name these notes. Draw lines to the keyboard.

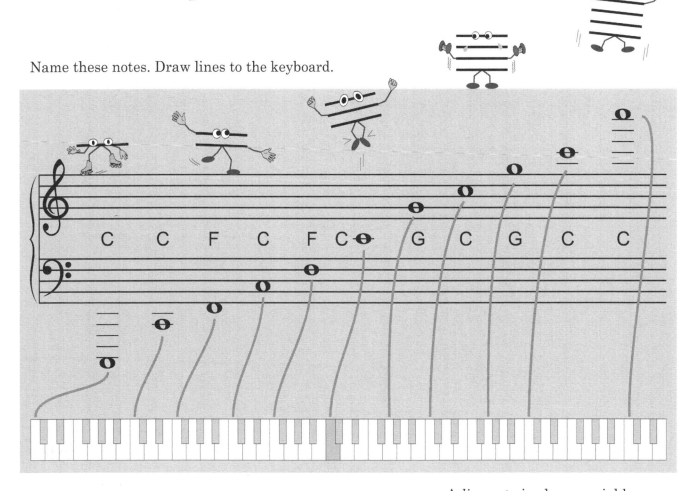

C   C   F   C   F   C   G   C   G   C   C

Write these melodic intervals.

*Write the intervals.*

A *line* note is always neighbors with a **space** note above and a **space** note below.

A *space* note is always neighbors with a **line** note above and a **line** note below.

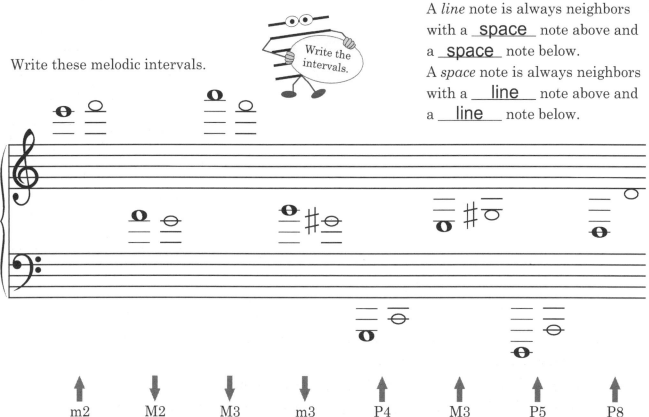

m2   M2   M3   m3   P4   M3   P5   P8

Doctor Mozart Music Theory Workbook, Answers for Level 2 & 3. © MMVIII, MMXV Machiko and Paul Christopher Musgrave. Published by April Avenue Music. www.DoctorMozart.com

# Circle of 5ths: Sharp Key Snail

Each of these notes is the tonic of a major scale. Name the notes. Write the number of sharps needed for each scale. Name the intervals between the notes.

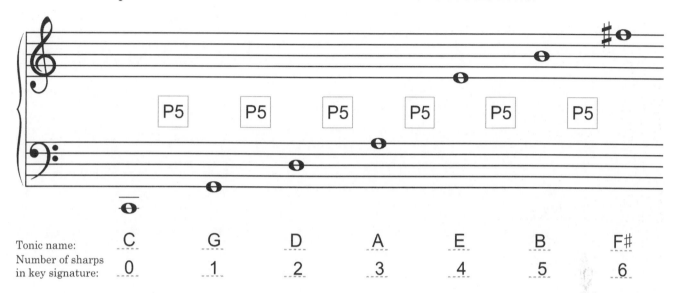

| | | | | | | | |
|---|---|---|---|---|---|---|---|
| Tonic name: | C | G | D | A | E | B | F# |
| Number of sharps in key signature: | 0 | 1 | 2 | 3 | 4 | 5 | 6 |

Does the snail contain all the tonic notes that are printed on the above staff? **Yes** Which tonic note comes after C? **G**

How many sharps are in the G major key signature? **1**

Look at the snail. Then complete this table.

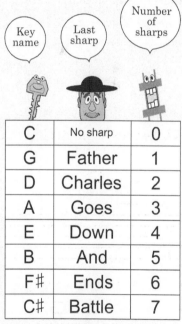

| Key name | Last sharp | Number of sharps |
|---|---|---|
| C | No sharp | 0 |
| G | Father | 1 |
| D | Charles | 2 |
| A | Goes | 3 |
| E | Down | 4 |
| B | And | 5 |
| F# | Ends | 6 |
| C# | Battle | 7 |

As the orange snail moves clockwise, each tonic note is a **P** 5 higher than the one before.

Each key signature has 1 **sharp** more than the previous key signature.

The new sharp is always for the **leading** note of the scale.

In the snail, which key has 3 sharps? **A** major. Which key has 4 sharps? **E** major.

Doctor Mozart Music Theory Workbook, Answers for Level 2 & 3. © MMVIII, MMXV Machiko and Paul Christopher Musgrave. Published by April Avenue Music. www.DoctorMozart.com

# Circle of 5ths: Flat Key Snail

Each of these notes is the tonic of a major scale. Name the notes. Write the number of flats needed for each scale. Name the intervals between the notes.

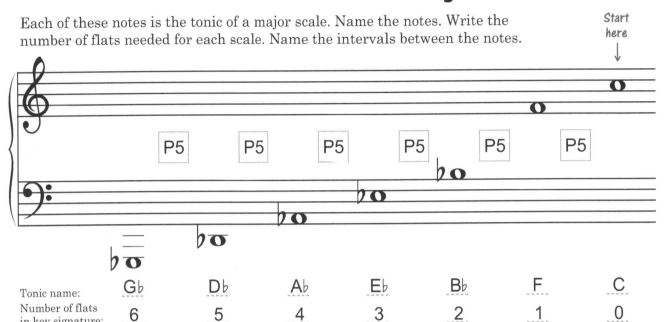

| Tonic name: | G♭ | D♭ | A♭ | E♭ | B♭ | F | C |
|---|---|---|---|---|---|---|---|
| Number of flats in key signature: | 6 | 5 | 4 | 3 | 2 | 1 | 0 |

Does the snail contain all the tonic notes that are printed on the above staff? __Yes__ Which tonic note comes after C? __F__
How many flats are in the F major key signature? __1__

Look at the snail. Then complete this table.

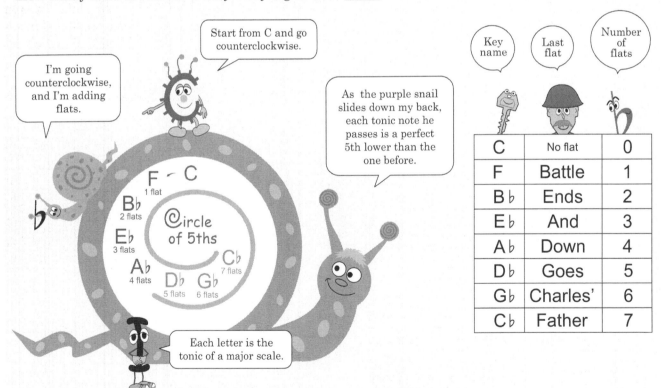

| Key name | Last flat | Number of flats |
|---|---|---|
| C | No flat | 0 |
| F | Battle | 1 |
| B♭ | Ends | 2 |
| E♭ | And | 3 |
| A♭ | Down | 4 |
| D♭ | Goes | 5 |
| G♭ | Charles' | 6 |
| C♭ | Father | 7 |

As the purple snail moves counterclockwise, each tonic note he passes is a __P5__ lower than the one before. Each key signature has 1 __flat__ more than the previous key signature.

The *second last* flat is always for the _____tonic_____ note of the scale.

In the snail, which key has 3 flats? __E♭__ major. Which key has 4 flats? __A♭__ major.

On this grand staff, what interval separates each note from the next? __P5__
Each note is the tonic of a major scale. Name the notes.
Write the number of sharps or flats needed for each scale.

Add sharps ↗

Start here

← Add flats

| Tonic name: | A♭ | E♭ | B♭ | F | C | G | D | A | E | B |
|---|---|---|---|---|---|---|---|---|---|---|
| Number of flats or sharps: | 4 | 3 | 2 | 1 | 0 | 1 | 2 | 3 | 4 | 5 |

Write the missing letters on the snail. Complete both tables.

Start from C.

Add flats ↙          Add sharps ↘

Circle of 5ths

Can you see how the tonic notes in the snail form a **circle of 5ths**?

| C | No flat | 0 |
|---|---|---|
| F | Battle | 1 |
| B♭ | Ends | 2 |
| E♭ | And | 3 |
| A♭ | Down | 4 |
| D♭ | Goes | 5 |
| G♭ | Charles' | 6 |
| C♭ | Father | 7 |

| C | No sharp | 0 |
|---|---|---|
| G | Father | 1 |
| D | Charles | 2 |
| A | Goes | 3 |
| E | Down | 4 |
| B | And | 5 |
| F♯ | Ends | 6 |
| C♯ | Battle | 7 |

In key signatures, flats are written in the reverse order from sharps.

**Battle Ends And Down Goes Charles Father.**

How can you use the circle of 5ths? Draw lines to the correct answers.

To add a sharp
To remove a flat          • move up a perfect 5th.

To add a flat
To remove a sharp          • move down a perfect 5th.

3

# More Musical Terms

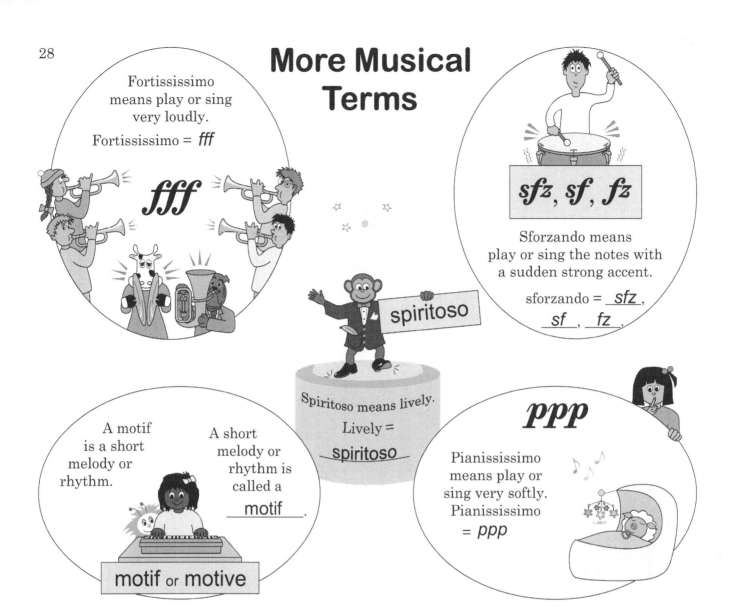

Fortississimo means play or sing very loudly.

Fortississimo = *fff*

*fff*

Sforzando means play or sing the notes with a sudden strong accent.

sforzando = __sfz__, __sf__, __fz__.

spiritoso

Spiritoso means lively.

Lively = __spiritoso__

*ppp*

Pianississimo means play or sing very softly.
Pianississimo = *ppp*

A motif is a short melody or rhythm.

A short melody or rhythm is called a __motif__.

motif or motive

Draw lines to match each sign or term with its meaning.

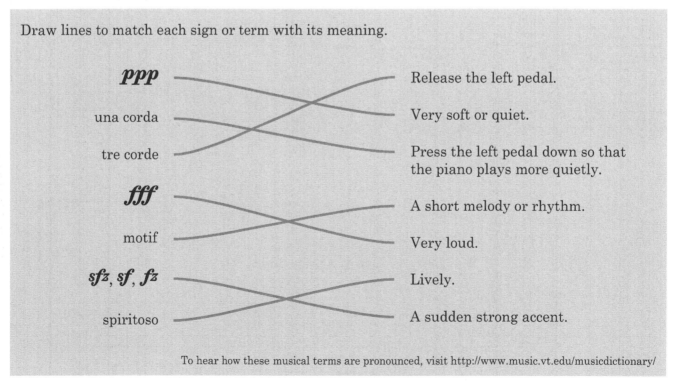

|  | |  |
|---|---|---|
| *ppp* | | Release the left pedal. |
| una corda | | Very soft or quiet. |
| tre corde | | Press the left pedal down so that the piano plays more quietly. |
| *fff* | | A short melody or rhythm. |
| motif | | Very loud. |
| *sfz, sf, fz* | | Lively. |
| spiritoso | | A sudden strong accent. |

To hear how these musical terms are pronounced, visit http://www.music.vt.edu/musicdictionary/

Doctor Mozart Music Theory Workbook, Answers for Level 2 & 3. © MMVIII, MMXV Machiko and Paul Christopher Musgrave. Published by April Avenue Music. www.DoctorMozart.com

# Expert Quiz

Write the correct key signature in each bar.
Write the major and minor tonic notes.
Name the major and minor keys.

| | | |
|---|---|---|
| 2♭ | 2♯ | 3♭ |
| B♭ major | D major | E♭ major |
| G minor | B minor | C minor |

| | | | |
|---|---|---|---|
| 3♯ | 4♭ | 4♯ | 5♯ |
| A major | A♭ major | E major | B major |
| F♯ minor | F minor | C♯ minor | G♯ minor |

Next, each note is the tonic of a minor scale. Write the key signatures. Name the key signatures.

C minor    C♯ minor    G minor    B minor

E minor    F♯ minor    F minor

Expert!

Tony

Name these intervals. Then on the right side of each staff, write the key signature that matches the accidentals. Name the major key. Write the primary triads.

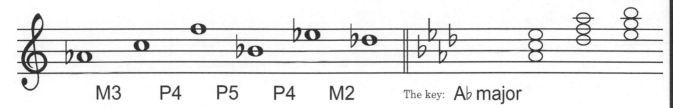

M3    P4    P5    P4    M2    The key: A♭ major

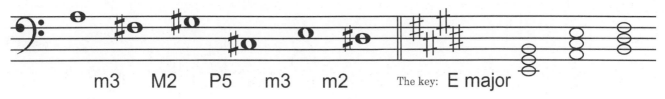

m3    M2    P5    m3    m2    The key: E major

3

Doctor Mozart Music Theory Workbook, Answers for Level 2 & 3.  © MMVIII, MMXV  Machiko and Paul Christopher Musgrave.    Published by April Avenue Music.    www.DoctorMozart.com

# Major Minor Scale Review

For each tonic note, write the correct key signature after the double bar line. Then write the relative minor scale, ascending and descending.

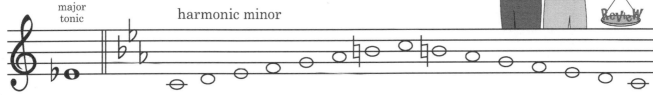

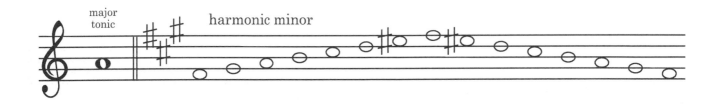

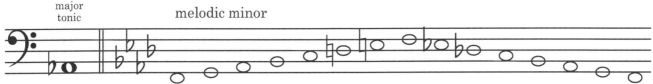

For each tonic note, write the correct key signature after the double bar line. Then write the relative major primary triads.

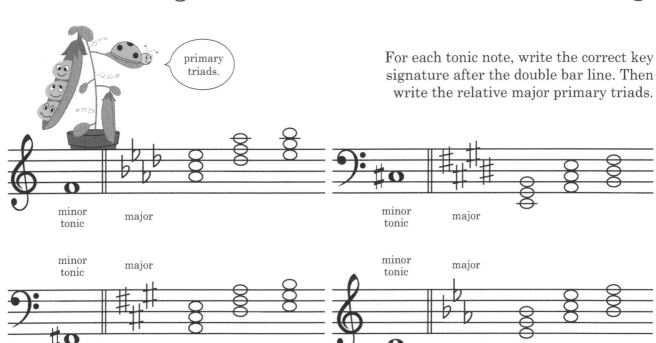

# Chord & Key Signature Quiz

Four triads are listed at left. The hats indicate major or minor. On each keyboard, write R, 3, and 5 to show the root, 3rd, and 5th of each triad. If the note is G, circle whatever you write on that key.

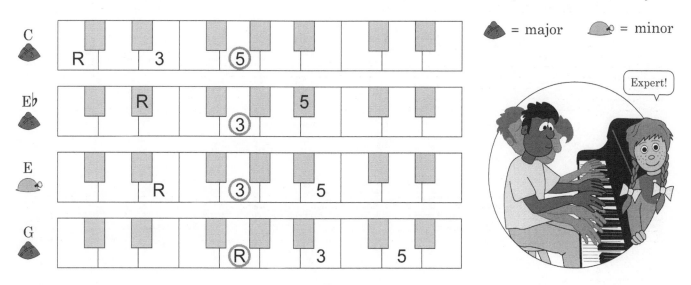

Complete each chord by writing a C. Name the chords. Remember, M = major, and m = minor.

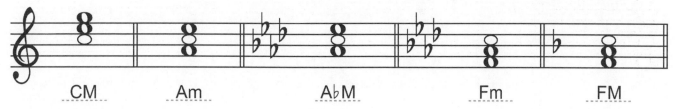

CM    Am    A♭M    Fm    FM

Next, the number on the left side of each keyboard tells you what key signature is needed. Circle the words that match each key signature. Label the required black keys. Label the major tonic using an upper case letter. Label the relative minor tonic using a lower case letter.

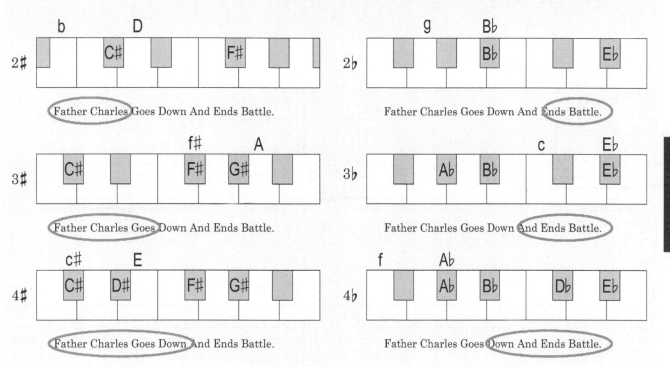

Doctor Mozart Music Theory Workbook, Answers for Level 2 & 3.  © MMVIII, MMXV Machiko and Paul Christopher Musgrave.    Published by April Avenue Music.    www.DoctorMozart.com

# Transposition

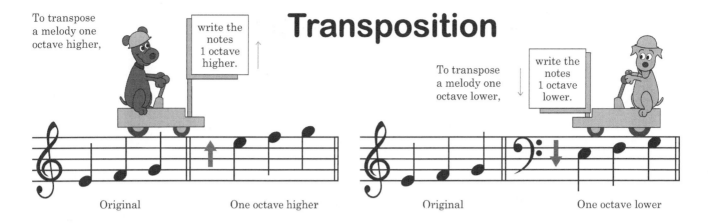

Transpose this melody one octave higher. Write it on the blank staff.

Next, at each green bracket, transpose up 1 octave. At each red bracket, transpose down 1 octave.

Doctor Mozart Music Theory Workbook, Answers for Level 2 & 3. © MMVIII, MMXV Machiko and Paul Christopher Musgrave. Published by April Avenue Music. www.DoctorMozart.com

# Repetition & Sequences

When a melody repeats itself exactly, we call that repetition.

When a melody repeats at a higher or lower pitch, we call that a sequence.

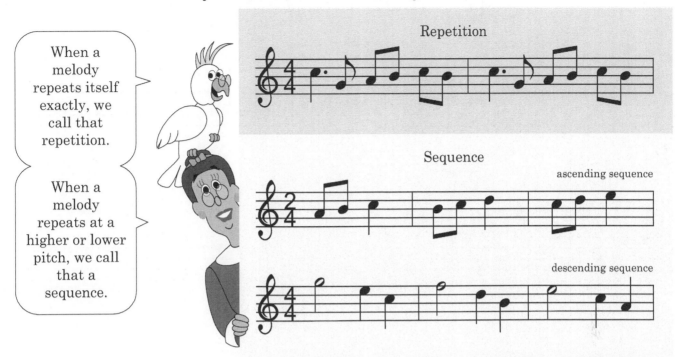

Repetition

Sequence

ascending sequence

descending sequence

In a sequence, the motif occurs at least 3 times, each time at a different pitch.

Next, write "R" for repetition and "S" for sequence. Draw a V bracket at each minor 2nd.

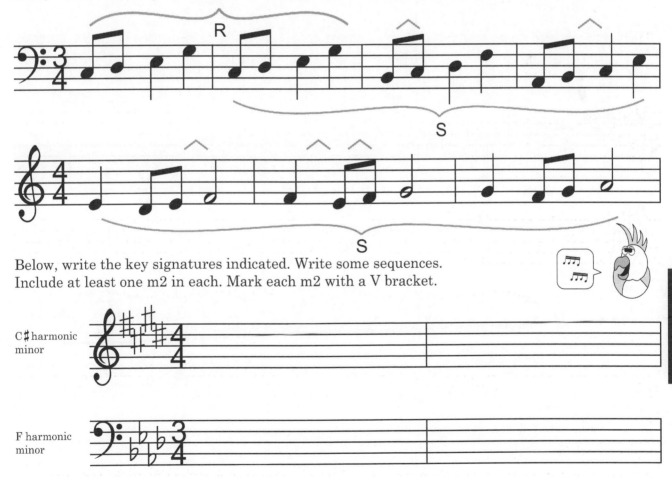

Below, write the key signatures indicated. Write some sequences. Include at least one m2 in each. Mark each m2 with a V bracket.

C♯ harmonic minor

F harmonic minor

Doctor Mozart Music Theory Workbook, Answers for Level 2 & 3.  © MMVIII, MMXV Machiko and Paul Christopher Musgrave.  Published by April Avenue Music.  www.DoctorMozart.com

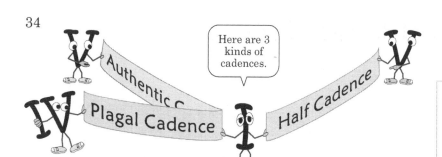

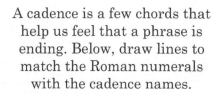

# Cadences

A cadence is a few chords that help us feel that a phrase is ending. Below, draw lines to match the Roman numerals with the cadence names.

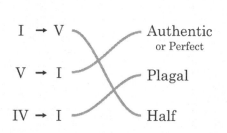

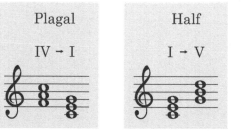

There are various kinds of half cadences, but they all end on V, like this: I –V or II – V.

Here are some cadences in C major. Write the Roman numerals. Name the cadences.

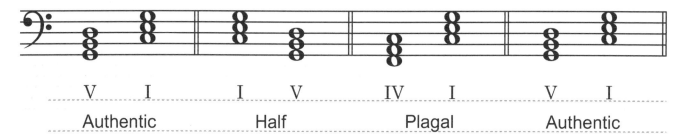

| V I | I V | IV I | V I |
|-----|-----|------|-----|
| Authentic | Half | Plagal | Authentic |

Write the key signatures, cadences, and Roman numerals.

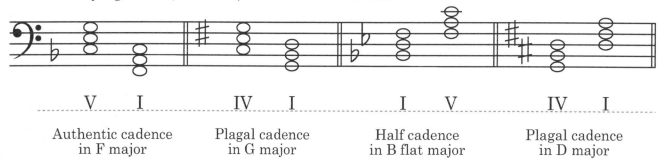

| V I | IV I | I V | IV I |
|-----|------|-----|------|
| Authentic cadence in F major | Plagal cadence in G major | Half cadence in B flat major | Plagal cadence in D major |

Each of these key signatures is for a major key. Write and name the cadences.

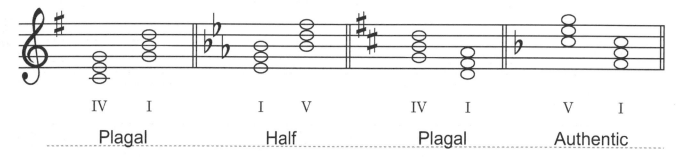

| IV I | I V | IV I | V I |
|------|-----|------|-----|
| Plagal | Half | Plagal | Authentic |

Doctor Mozart Music Theory Workbook, Answers for Level 2 & 3.  © MMVIII, MMXV  Machiko and Paul Christopher Musgrave.    Published by April Avenue Music.    www.DoctorMozart.com

# What is an Upbeat?

Some tunes do not start from the first beat. Instead, they start *before* the first bar. That's called an upbeat, or anacrusis.

Another word for upbeat is _____anacrusis_____.
Number the beats below this staff.

Notice that the last bar has only 3 beats. This is because the upbeat makes us feel that a 4th beat would start a new phrase.

Next, in each example, write some upbeat notes, and one or more notes in the last bar. The upbeat plus the notes in the last bar should add to a full bar of time. Name each key signature as a major key. Draw a V bracket at each m2.

> In this example, the last bar should have only 2 beats because the other 2 beats are used at the beginning.

Teacher: These are just examples.

**Key Signature Review**

On the following staff, write the key signatures shown by the gray keys on the keyboards. Write the major and relative minor tonic notes.

# Adding Rests to Complete a Bar

This bar contains only one 16th note. How can we add rests to complete the bar?

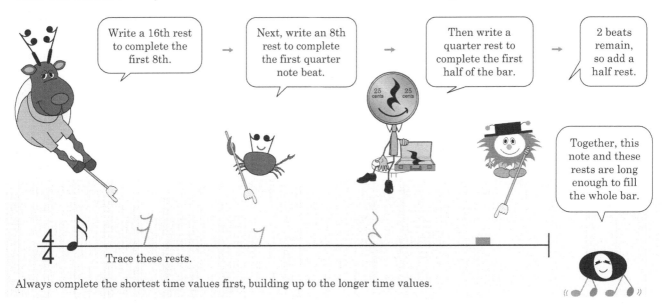

Trace these rests.

Always complete the shortest time values first, building up to the longer time values.

Write rests to complete each bar.

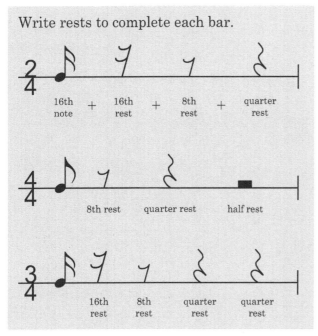

It is common to combine the 2nd and 3rd beats in one *note*, but not in one *rest*. Instead, write 2 rests.

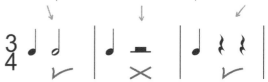

Write rests to complete these bars.

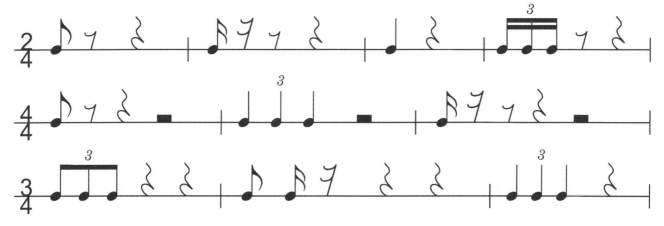

Doctor Mozart Music Theory Workbook, Answers for Level 2 & 3.   © MMVIII, MMXV  Machiko and Paul Christopher Musgrave.   Published by April Avenue Music.   www.DoctorMozart.com

# Starting with Rests

This bar has only one note at the end.
How can we add rests to complete the bar?

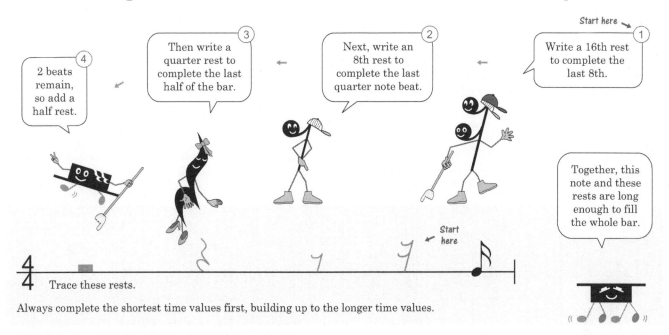

Trace these rests.

Always complete the shortest time values first, building up to the longer time values.

Write rests to complete each bar.

quarter rest + quarter rest. + 8th rest

Do not use half rests in 3/4 time.
Quarter rests are easier to read.

ADD BACKWARD

Write rests to complete these bars.

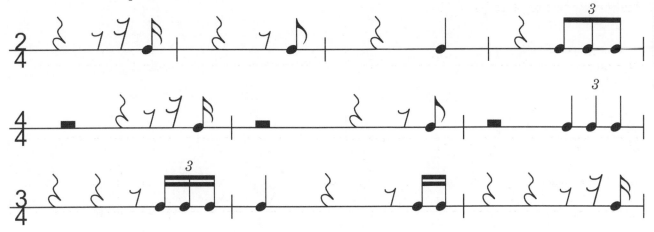

Doctor Mozart Music Theory Workbook, Answers for Level 2 & 3.  © MMVIII, MMXV  Machiko and Paul Christopher Musgrave.    Published by April Avenue Music.    www.DoctorMozart.com

3

# Triad Inversions

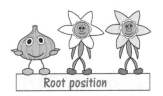
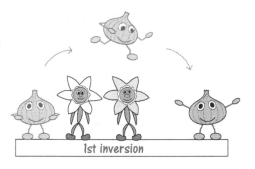
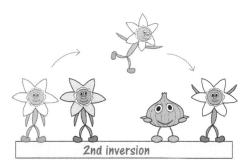

Root position     1st inversion     2nd inversion

To invert a triad, move the bottom note up one octave. On these keyboards, write R, 3, and 5, to show the inversions. Draw arrows to show how each bottom note moves up one octave.

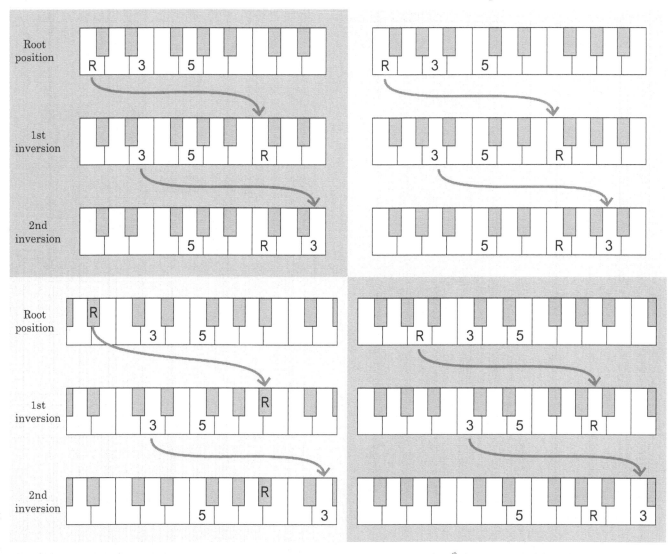

Write the inversions for each chord. Draw arrows to show how each bottom note moves up one octave. Name the root position (RP) and inversions.

RP = Root Position.     R = the Root note of the triad.

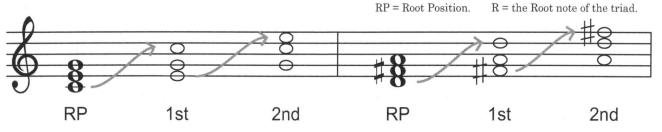

RP     1st     2nd     RP     1st     2nd

Doctor Mozart Music Theory Workbook, Answers for Level 2 & 3. © MMVIII, MMXV Machiko and Paul Christopher Musgrave.    Published by April Avenue Music.    www.DoctorMozart.com

# INVERSION

## QUIZ

Root position

1st inversion

2nd inversion

Invert each triad on the staff and on the keyboard.
Draw arrows. Name the inversions as RP, 1st, and 2nd.

Doctor Mozart Music Theory Workbook, Answers for Level 2 & 3. © MMVIII, MMXV Machiko and Paul Christopher Musgrave. Published by April Avenue Music. www.DoctorMozart.com

# Broken Chords

In a solid chord, all the notes are played at the same time. In a broken chord, the notes are played separately, one at a time.

This is a solid chord.

This is a broken chord.

The notes are played together.

The notes are played separately.

Name the chords, cadences, and keys.

B♭ major — I V — half cadence

D major — V I — authentic cadence

E major — IV I — plagal cadence

A♭ major — V I — authentic cadence

C minor — V I — authentic cadence

E minor — I V — half cadence

Write and name two major key cadences. Include some broken triads.

# Major Minor Scale Quiz

Each colored key is the tonic note of a *major* scale. Name the relative *minor* at left. Label the notes of the harmonic minor scale.

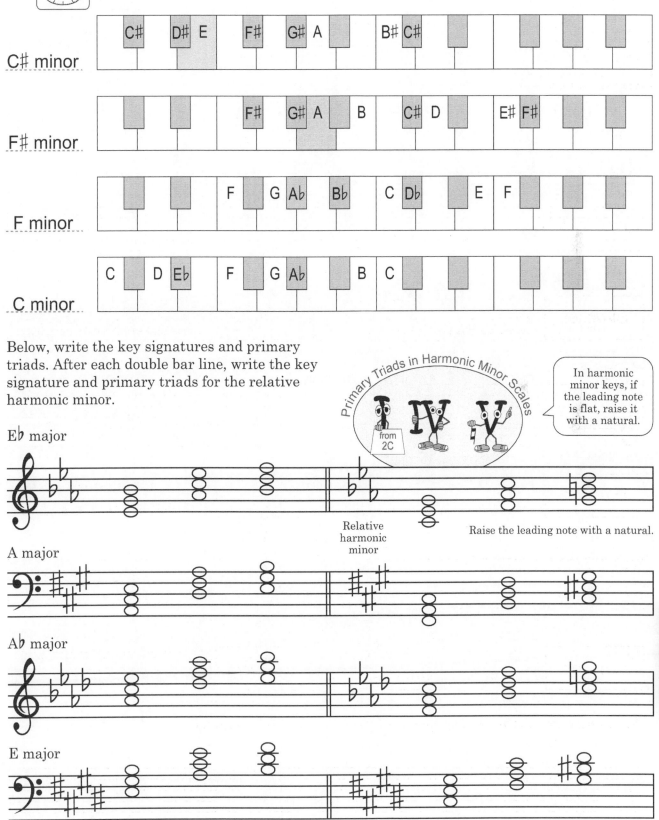

**C♯ minor** — C♯ D♯ E F♯ G♯ A B♯ C♯

**F♯ minor** — F♯ G♯ A B C♯ D E♯ F♯

**F minor** — F G A♭ B♭ C D♭ E F

**C minor** — C D E♭ F G A♭ B C

Below, write the key signatures and primary triads. After each double bar line, write the key signature and primary triads for the relative harmonic minor.

Primary Triads in Harmonic Minor Scales

I IV V (from 2C)

In harmonic minor keys, if the leading note is flat, raise it with a natural.

E♭ major

Relative harmonic minor

Raise the leading note with a natural.

A major

A♭ major

E major

Doctor Mozart Music Theory Workbook, Answers for Level 2 & 3. © MMVIII, MMXV Machiko and Paul Christopher Musgrave. Published by April Avenue Music. www.DoctorMozart.com

3

# Harmonic & Melodic Minor

Review

In a harmonic minor scale, raise the leading note with an accidental.

Here, each printed note is the 7th note of a harmonic minor scale. Write the tonic notes and key signatures. Name the keys.

E minor   D minor   B minor   F# minor

G minor   C# minor   C minor   F minor

Next, each bar contains the 6th and 7th notes of an ascending melodic minor scale. Write the tonic note and the key signature for each.

B minor   C minor   E minor

F minor   D minor   C# minor

Below, each bar contains the 7th and 6th notes of a descending melodic minor scale. Write the tonic and the key signature for each. Remember, the tonic must be one M2 above the leading note.

In melodic minor scales, raise the 6th and 7th notes on the way up, but not on the way down.

6  7  1
6  7  1

E minor   D minor   B minor

C# minor   C minor   F# minor

# Transposition & Triplets

Transpose these notes onto the blank staff.
Remember to write the key signatures.

Complete each bar with either 3 eighth notes, or one eighth note triplet group. Number the beats.

Complete each bar with either 3 sixteenth notes, or one sixteenth note triplet group. Number the beats.

 Rests

 Inversions

Cadences

Write rests to complete each bar. Number the beats.

A weak beat rest should never continue through a strong beat.

The following chords are tonic triads. Invert them. Color each root note red.
Write RP, 1st, or 2nd, to show the position of each chord. Name the key signatures.

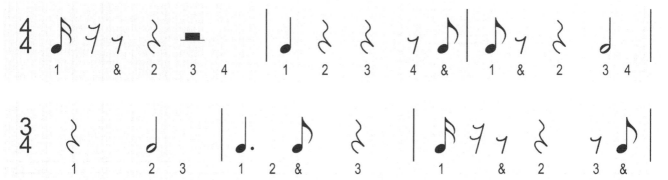

F minor    RP    1st    2nd        F major    RP    1st    2nd

E minor    RP    1st    2nd        E major    RP    1st    2nd

Write the correct clefs. Write each cadence in the relative harmonic minor key. Number the chords.

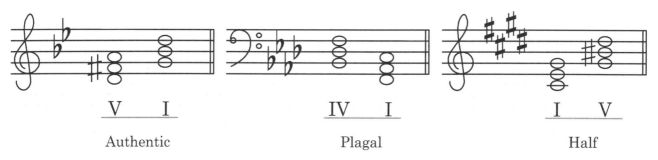

V   I                    IV   I                    I   V

Authentic                Plagal                   Half

Doctor Mozart Music Theory Workbook, Answers for Level 2 & 3.  © MMVIII, MMXV  Machiko and Paul Christopher Musgrave.    Published by April Avenue Music.    www.DoctorMozart.com

# Name The Chord Notes

Number these chords with Roman numerals. Then label each treble staff note with R, 3, or 5, to show whether it is the root, 3rd, or 5th. Write an X above any notes that do not belong to the chord.

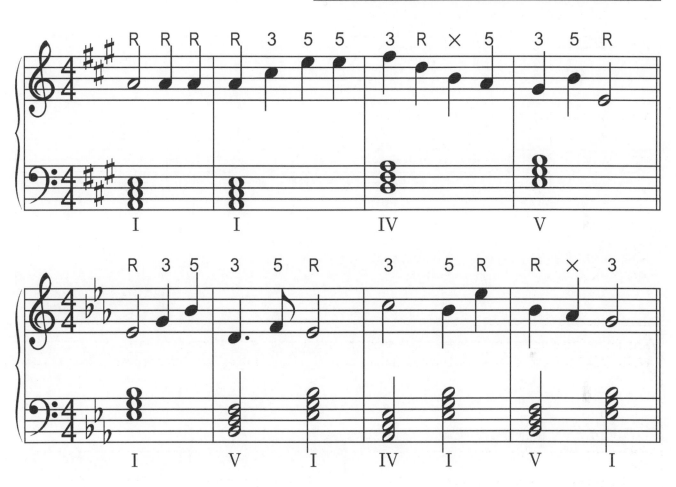

Name each triad. Draw a line between each pair of triads to show which notes are the same. Remember, M means major, and m means minor.

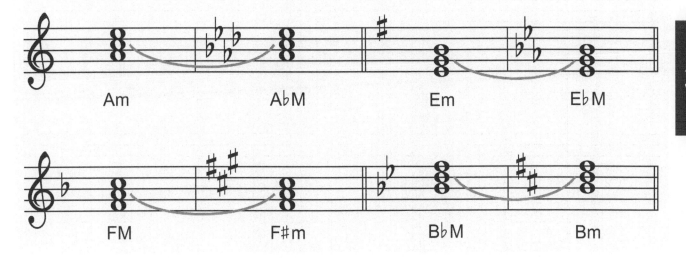

Doctor Mozart Music Theory Workbook, Answers for Level 2 & 3.  © MMVIII, MMXV  Machiko and Paul Christopher Musgrave.    Published by April Avenue Music.    www.DoctorMozart.com

# Multipurpose Notes

Review!

Each of these notes is the 3rd of a tonic triad. Write the key signatures. Complete the triads.
Name the triads. M means major, and m means minor.

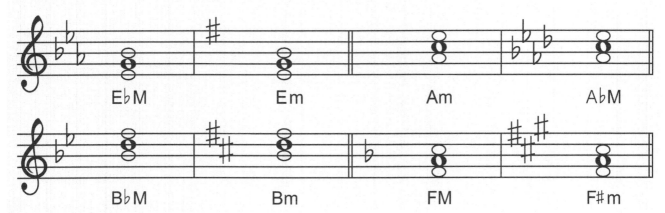

EbM    Em    Am    AbM

BbM    Bm    FM    F#m

Next, each phrase describes the note on the staff
in a different way. Fill in the blanks.

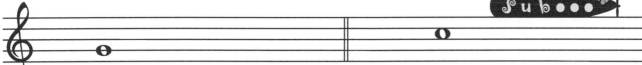

V in __C__ major.
IV in __D__ major.
I in __G__ major.
The root of the __G__ major triad.
The 3rd of the __E__ minor triad.
The 3rd of the __Eb__ major triad.
The 5th of the __C__ major triad.

V in __F__ major.
IV in __G__ major.
I in __C__ major.
The root of the __C__ major triad.
The 3rd of the __A__ minor triad.
The 3rd of the __Ab__ major triad.
The 5th of the __F__ major triad.

V in __G__ major.
IV in __A__ major.
I in __D__ major.
The root of the __D__ major triad.
The 3rd of the __B__ minor triad.
The 3rd of the __Bb__ major triad.
The 5th of the __G__ major triad.

V in __D__ major.
IV in __E__ major.
I in __A__ major.
The root of the __A__ major triad.
The 3rd of the __F#__ minor triad.
The 3rd of the __F__ major triad.
The 5th of the __D__ major triad.

Doctor Mozart Music Theory Workbook, Answers for Level 2 & 3.  © MMVIII, MMXV  Machiko and Paul Christopher Musgrave.    Published by April Avenue Music.    www.DoctorMozart.com

# Doctor Mozart Music Theory Workbook
## Answers for Level 2 and 3

**Level 2A**

Version 1.1.0
or higher.

Ledger notes
Whole steps up and down
The C, F, and G major scales
Eighth notes
Dotted half notes
Primary and secondary accents
Time signatures

**2A**

**Level 2B**

Version 1.0.5
or higher.

Major and minor 2nds and 3rds
Perfect 4ths and 5ths
White key accidentals
Major and minor triads
Primary triads on I, IV, and V in C, F, and G major
2/8, 3/8, and 4/8 time signatures
Eighth rests

**2B**

**Level 2C**

Version 1.0.5
or higher.

Major and minor 6ths and 7ths
Unisons and octaves
Key signatures
The D major and B flat major scales
Minor scales and primary triads
16th notes and rests
Dotted quarter notes

**2C**

**Level 3**

Version 1.0.1
or higher.

Key signatures up to 4 flats
    and 5 sharps
The circle of 5ths
Melodic minor scales
Intervals on ledger notes
Triad inversions
Transposition
Cadences

Dotted eighth notes
Common time and cut time
Triplets
Compound time signatures
Upbeats
Adding rests to complete a bar
Repetition and sequences
Musical terminology

**3**

Doctor Mozart Music Theory Workbook, Answers for Level 2 & 3.   © MMVIII, MMXV  Machiko and Paul Christopher Musgrave.   Published by April Avenue Music.   www.DoctorMozart.com

10894868R00092

Printed in Great Britain
by Amazon.co.uk, Ltd.,
Marston Gate.